HOLLYWOOD

B. S.

BY

MICHAEL G. UVA

IF THIS BUSINESS IS THAT EASY...

THEY WOULD HIRE THEIR RELATIVES!

HOLLYWOOD

BEHIND THE SCENES

This industry is fun. Sure, there is a lot of hard work with long shooting days, under some extreme conditions. Still, I love it. There are so many pros and cons. Many more pros for a person of my ilk. In this book I hope to answer some of your questions without getting myself sued. In today's world, as you may know, I might get sued for saying, *good morning, you look lovely!* (How dare I?)

Oh well!

I'm guessing you bought this book to find out what really goes on behind the scenes.

Where to start? How about the beginning. No, not Hollywood's beginning; everybody already knows those stories. I'm going to start with a simple beginning. First, let me tell you this, it has been one hell of a ride so far. So, with no further ado, let me repeat the phrase from a famous actress, buckle up, it's going to be one hell of a ride. Or wait… was it? Fasten your seatbelts; it's going to be a bumpy night.

No, wait, it was… I don't remember, but you can see how myths may have been born in Hollywood. Now, I am going to give you the straight skinny, the inside dope, as I see it, lived it, and loved it. My firsthand accounting. I have added a few personal stories… that I can prove in court.

Other stories have come from a lot of straight shooters I have known for decades. I find these stories funny as hell. I hope you do, too. Some of these stories might sound unbelievable. I would always think, there is just no way that went down that way! OMG, are you B.S.-ing me? You be the judge… and jury!

Notice about Hollywood!

A fairytale has two types of beginnings in Hollywood. One begins with, once upon a time… and the other begins with, this is no shit!

STORIES IN THIS BOOK

Bob (Guaranteed accurate!)

While prepping a shooting location at a psychiatric hospital, I witnessed our location manager (Bob) knock on a thick steel door. The door had a one-foot glass square window. The location manager yelled a bit loud at the orderly through the thick glass, *Hi, I'm Bob, the location manager. I need to return inside and look for an additional area to film in for a just-added shot.* The orderly on the other side quietly answered, *please speak lower and repeat your question.* Being who he is, Bob crouched at the knees, lowering himself about a foot or so, and yelled loudly at the window once again. *I need to come inside again to scout.* In utter amazement, the orderly just shook his head from side to side and then answered, *you know what, you need to be a resident of this place,* and then buzzed him in.

Boys' Town

Boys' Town is an authentic combination of lust and debauchery. It really exists. Located in Mexico just across the state line from Nuevo Laredo, Texas. When I first arrived there, I noticed that the entire compound was about the size of only a few city blocks. The encampment was surrounded by a very thick, high wall. On top of the wall were shards of broken glass. I only saw one entrance and exit with a guard gate. At that time, I felt like I had entered the destroyed city of Sodom and Gomorrah.

For a first-time attendee, such as myself, it was overwhelming. There were rows and rows of tiny little bars lined up next to each other. Every single hole-in-the-wall bar had a variety of satisfaction for one's sexual stimuli. Up until that day, I did not know that there even existed so many varieties and variations of sexual indulgence. I remember thinking, Mike, don't look, but like the words from an old Ray Stevens song, "The Streak" went like this: don't look Ethel! It was too late. The genie had left the bottle at the speed of sight. I no longer possessed any vestige of a virgin-like mind. My life was changed immeasurably for the short few hours other crew members and I were there. I saw things I wished I had never seen to this day. At first, you might think going into these dark places is quite exciting. But the memories you take will stay with you for the rest of your life. It has been said, "If it's your cup of tea…" Well, I decided to drink water after that. To quote a line from "The Wizard of Oz," *I have a feeling we're not in Kansas anymore!*

Lava - This is a Fact! Not fiction!

Picking the Lava pebbles out of our tennis shoe bottoms before leaving Helo, Hawaii.

(Reason, Do Not Take Any Lava. None!)

This is an old Hawaiian tradition, I am told. Maybe true, maybe not. But I was not taking any chances. One set person was hacking away at the plants (Not allowed in the sanctuary where we were filming) to make it clear view for the camera to get a better shot. He was told not to do it, but he didn't listen. That Night, after we wrapped up and drove away from the filming location, we encountered an accident. It was the set person's van. I kid you not, a horse had fallen off a roadside cliff and landed squarely on the hood of his moving van, causing him to crash and break a leg. (So, you see… no pebbles for me.)

Petty (Guaranteed accurate!)

In a particular chewing gum commercial, the client rep from the gum company wanted the craft service person fired. Why, you ask? The crafty person had the Gaul to lay out a wonderful spread of food and snacks. The table, fit for a king and queen, had everything, including an assortment of the famed gum product being filmed. But low and behold, a few sticks of a competitor's gum were mixed into this feast. The audacity! How dare they!

Embarrassed on a movie set?

The Chandler!

Pacino!

Squat in the field!

Once Bitten - The Fart! (Guaranteed true!)

Suppose you have seen the movie mentioned above. In that case, it is where Jim, in an extreme close-up, stands outside of the school building, facing the courtyard and explaining what's been happening to him to his girlfriend. It was a nonunion shoot that I was working on at the time. We always needed more crew members. I was asked if I could lend a hand and work the slates/the sticks to help the camera assistant. This was a widespread practice in those days… being nonunion and all.

Rolling was called. I slammed the sticks together after the camera was rolling. Instead of running out of this tight scene to hide around the far-away corner, I merely spun around, stepped out of the frame, and faced the wall, not looking at the actors. And then… gastric acids started tearing up my stomach.

Jim was in the middle of giving one of his best performances while I was dying in pain as the pressure grew. Jim was just about to say something when the gas bubble… popped. OMG… WTF!

I farted loud and hard. Jim, being the consummate professional he was, merely waved one hand before his face and kept talking until he went into a tirade of his most hilarious jokes. Cut was finally hollered, and a back-to-one reset was beckoned. Frozen like a statue, I stood there facing the wall. (There was no frigg'en way I was going to turn around.)

Horseshoe Crab in A Toilet (Guaranteed accurate!)

In Florida, they have a crustacean called a horseshoe crab. Scary as all get out looking. The roommate crew members knew that a particular crew member would always race into their rented apartment after wrapping and running for the only downstairs toilet. He always needed 15 minutes of quiet time, day after day. Unbeknownst to the now almost quietly resting crew member, the roommates he was staying with had stuck a live horseshoe crab in the toilet, pinchers facing upwards.

He looked down and within seconds the once-racing crewmember about to land on the throne screamed. A loud commotion was heard suddenly coming from inside the small palace. This was followed by a banging off the walls as the door opened. A wide-eyed man ran down the hall, swearing. The two mischievous crewmembers were lying on the floor laughing their asses off.

Mensa Smart! (Guaranteed true!)

During a quick re-dress of the set, a crewmember was speaking with a famous aged actor.

The performer was lamenting how he had lost several actor friends over the last few years. The less-than-Mensa society crewmember blurted out, "hell, before this show, I thought you were dead, too!" I almost choked!

Days of Polaroid Cameras (Guaranteed accurate!)

Someone… had gotten their hands on the script person's Polaroid camera (which was mainly used in the olden days of yore to take a photo of an actor's make-up or the set set-up for matching purposes between each take.) Well, this someone had taken a nice clear picture of cow poo. After letting it develop, they would push the photo back into the camera cartridge slot. Lo and behold, the very next shot would deliver that same photo. I am told that other images of other body parts were also accidentally reloaded. (lion and tigers and snakes, oh my!)

Fish Under the Passenger Seat (Guaranteed actual!)

Several crewmembers were pissed off at a smart-ass PA (Production Assistant) on a nonunion shoot. The PA was hired to drive the production cube truck (a small U-Haul-type moving truck) from California to Las Vegas, Nevada. It all went well on the drive there. After three days in the hot sun, the P.A. driver could not stand to get into the cube truck's cab. It smelled too high heaven. But the P.A. had to drive the smelly truck back to California, unload it completely, and then turn it back into the truck rental company.

Several days later, the production company renting the truck received a vast cleaning bill. The first item listed was a smelly dead fish found taped up under the passenger seat!

Running to the Stage Phone to Get the Next Job

Long before cell phones, everyone used the stage phone at lunch to get their next job. Here is what happened: Hey Johnny, there's a work call for you. Unsuspecting, Jonny swiftly ran to the phone and pressed the receiver's handset to his ear. It had been primed with a thick mound of Vaseline spread all over the earpiece rim. Ah… yuk!

Bull-Chit Stories Said to Crews (I heard 99.7% of these!)

It's just two people sitting at a table.

Let's roll on the rehearsal.

One more time.

She will be ready in 5.

Sure, we have permission to film here.

The checks are in the mail.

There won't be any double-up days.

Today's going to be a short one.

We only need the crane for one shot.

We talked about this on the scout.

We're like a family here.

We're wrapping up by ten P.M.

We'll get you on the next one!

You don't need last looks; it's just a rehearsal!

Snake

Sometimes, the prop department would tie a string to a rubber snake and put it under the craft service table. The string was slowly pulled when a crew member approached the crafty table.

Lifted (Guaranteed true!)

Someone had raised the lead actors' fancy new car about 1/8 inch off the ground. After wrap time, the actor got in and started his car. When he put it in gear, the engine revved, but it wouldn't go anywhere! He stopped it, got out, and walked around the car. Finding nothing, he got back in and tried again. Same results. So, he got out again and checked under the hood! (WTF) Finally, a few crew members watching him ran over and explained that they had seen this problem before. It is said to have happened on these models before on these types of new cars. All he needed to do was get back in and let a few crewmembers push the new car a few feet to re-engage his drive-to-shaft-go-gear. He did what was asked. It appeared to fix the perceived problem. So, he drove off happily! But the next Night, it was much colder outside… and low and behold, the problem had returned.

Middle Sticks

The camera assistant will always put a slate up in front of the camera lens after the camera begins to roll. Sometimes, it may have been out of focus, or only half the slate was seen in the frame. So, at the end of the scene, the assistant will quickly thrust the slate in the frame, this time upside down, and call out tail sticks, end sticks, or end slate!

Every so often, a newbie comes along who is a punk. The newbie is now instructed to rush in, hold the slate squarely in front of the camera's lens, bang the sticks together, and loudly call out the middle stick… during an intense love scene that is being filmed. (There are no such thing as middle sticks.) The unloved newbie is now flipping burgers at Jack' n the Box. No, I'm just kidding… it's MacDonald's!

Ice Cold

Someone asked the newbie to go to the igloo cooler and grab him an ice water. Opening the ice chest, he screamed loudly as a rubber snake flew out at his face. It was rigged to attack whenever it was opened.

The Sign

Someone had put up a sign at the crafty table just before lunch. The sign read: Production had set up a room in the extras' holding area so a nurse could drug test the crew members after lunch. You could see people's heads snap as they read the sign. Many just quietly wandered off the set when lunch was called minutes later. (The rumor is that there was not enough food for the entire crew!)

Milky Way Commercial (Guaranteed actual!)

It was lunch. We had been filming a bunch of actors all morning long. They would look straight into the camera lens and moan a big, heartfelt, mmm! This was accomplished while broadcasting a big smile. After lunch, as the crewmembers wandered back in, they flipped the camera on. They mimicked all the actors' winning performances from the morning. We knew the Director would see his crew's face during his daily rushes the next day. (The day before recordings on film, now processed and ready to be reviewed) Oddly enough, I got paid over 6K for that one joke. (You see, I had somehow, unknowingly, made it into the actual commercial being shown)

Sometimes, someone… (Guaranteed true! I was there.)

I am told there is a running joke that some crew members sneak something in the background during every take. I had heard that in one movie, a five-foot plaster yard angel in the background would always be looking straight at the camera—even during a reverse shot, a side shot, or even an overhead shot! Who were these Bastards?

Honk

Someone had wired the Director's car horn to honk every time he stepped on his brake after he put it in gear.

Cheese Pull

We have all seen the fantastic cheese pull in a pizza commercial. It shows how moist, creamy, and stretchy the cheese is. These perfect pizzas are usually painstakingly made by an experienced home economist. (A.k.a. The Chef.) Sometimes, it takes hours to make what is called the Hero product. It's the best way to show the world how fantastic their product is. After hours of preparation, the home economist raced out with the perfect pizza. She tripped! The pizza flew tumbling through the air and somehow landed with the cheese side down. The entire set went as quiet as house mice while the Director's face froze in distress. The Home economist yelled out "April Fools" (because it was) and called for the real hero pizza to come to set. (I awarded her 10 points!)

Old Time Movie Set Sayings!

It's a big day ahead; we're already two hours behind.

Do it right or do it twice!

Do your job, and we won't have any problems!

Does that phone have GPS? Great, then use it to find your way back to work!

Don't run. It looks like you forgot something!

Don't get married. Just find someone that you hate and then buy them a house!

Even Superman needs some alone time in the phone booth.

Give a specific crewmember a bowling ball and put them in a small room without doors or windows. They will either lose it, break it or try to have sex with it.

Having you on the job is like sending two outstanding crew members' home.

Hell, I can call this job in.

Hey buddy, the work's over here.

Hey, Meat Rocket!

How long will it take to set up the crane?

Answer by the Crane driver:

By myself; 10 minutes. Give me 45 minutes if you help.

I don't know what you know but I do know what you forgot.

I don't mind working hard, but I do mind working stupid.

I have seen better films on teeth.

I have seen it done better... but I've never seen it done slower.

I have been working in this studio longer than any of the toilets.

Exposed

Many years ago, all the recently exposed films (Before digital) were removed from the cameras and put into a unique black bag. This bag was then sealed into a round metal canister. All this work was accomplished in a pitch-black room. (Called the changing room) Finally, after several minutes, a brand-new assistant cameraperson emerged, with both arms loaded with the last fifteen work hours of freshly exposed film. It was to be rushed to the lavatory for development. Just one more step… OMG, he tripped and dropped all the cans, which popped open, exposing the can's contents. Upon closer inspection, several empty film core rolls and a few strips of already old, used, exposed film (basically, trash film) had been placed inside the metal can for effect. It worked. Upon realizing that they had been had, everyone took a breath in at the same time! Finally, the Director smiled and called out, thanks for a tremendous first-day crew! (I had to give him 10 points as well!)

Truths or Fiction when a Cell Phone Goes Off

Everyone on the working set turns toward the annoying sound with angry faces. The wrongdoer follows suit, turns, and investigates the far distance while slowly and quietly pressing the off button on the phone, unseen. (Whew! Dodged that bullet)

Late One Night

A production assistant told me that he had fallen asleep late one Night while leaning against the stage's side entry door, waiting for the red light to extinguish and allow entry. When he opened his eyes, he saw two famous actors waiting patiently. The PA's only word out of his mouth was, "Amen." Then, not skipping a beat, it will only be a few more seconds, guys." A moment later, the red light turned off. They both smiled as they passed him while he held the door open.

A Union Crewmember

One Night, during the last strike, a crewmember moonlighted to earn some money on a nonunion show. The person complained about the union's medical insurance. The look the person got from his nonunion comrades was, "You Have Medical Insurance?"

So, It Is Also Said!

The Director asked the first A.D. if the eight grips could push the giant crane faster? The crane grip answered. Nine women can't make a baby in one month!

Never run; if they wanted it sooner, they should have asked for it earlier.

The Director of photography was told directly to his face to calm down; the crew could only move as fast as the Director would change his mind.

A pissed-off gaffer told the Director, We're not happy until you're not happy!

Book of lies - book of lies… was once called out by a very seasoned P.A. as he handed out the revised call sheet!

I am still determining who coined this testimonial, but I have heard several versions of this tale over the years. It's not the time it takes to take the takes… it's the time it takes between the takes, but it takes the time it takes to take the takes! Clear as mud!

Someone told me that they had overheard this conversation. The UPM asks why the role of 1/2 CTO Gel costs the same as a roll of Full CTO? A fast-thinking grip answered that they had to slice it much thinner, so it took longer. UPM: Oh, thanks. Then he walked away.

The Director asks if we can make that happen. The critical grip answers that we can do anything you can afford!

The young UPM calls out to the grip. The script doesn't have a dance scene, so why do we need the dance floor? The seasoned female dolly grip just drops her head! (Dance floors are sheets of plywood used to smooth a rough area to roll the dolly on.)

While dropping a steel plate to crush an object being filmed, the Director wanted a heavier steel plate so it would fall faster. A voice yelled out; it doesn't work that way. The Director screams, who said that!? The voice yelled back, Newton!

A homeowner whose yard was being filmed told a specific big-time newspaper reporter on the location, did you know they have a special trailer where you can get almost anything to eat? It's called a honey-wagon. (Supposably, the homeowner's quote was published.) (A honey-wagon is where one goes to do their business… usually after they eat elsewhere)

A pissed-off Director of Photography asked the lamp operator, is there anything you can do fast? The operator answered quickly, Yep, I get tired real fast!

How to make it in Hollywood: Show concern and take no action.

A prop person supposedly told the Director that any machine is a smoke machine if you misuse it.

The Brothel (I ain't saying nothing)

A small bell rang as five crew members entered, and the doors opened. There were over a dozen scantily clad, sexily dressed, stiletto-heeled women. It was like finding a box of assorted ice cream for this crew on a hot August day in the desert. There were tall, small, and large-breasted women, from the tiny to the women with big... aspirations. Each one of the women was perfectly made up. Sexuality at its finest, that is, if you're into that sort of thing.

The self-appointed leader, stoic, decided to drink at the contained bar until the crew had finished their… uh… let's say "desserts." The indifferent one sat patiently enjoying his average bourbon drink, one-part Seagram's Seven, two parts 7-Up. From out of nowhere, a very large Anna Nicole Smith lookalike approached. She was fully decked out in a black sheer bodysuit. She wore a silk push-up bra while standing upon six-inch-stiletto heels. This was topped off with Texas-style, big blond hair. At that very point in time, he knew that he was going to indulge! (So, he's not an Oaktree.)

After School Special (It's Movie Code!)

This story has been repeated many times on the down low. It is said that some "film type" people had made a porno flick. (Six flicks.) Like many things in life, I am told, your first time doing anything, you're in amazement. The second time is more accessible. By flick #3, the film person was now an old salt. By flick #6, the same film person was finished. Done. Kaput! Don't ever call me again, I don't know you! Or so it is said.

Here is how the story goes… I am told. On the very first job, a call was received. This person was asked to travel to the San Francisco area and make what was called "an after-school special." At first glance, this film person thought it was a real after-school special. It was later explained that this was NO after-school special. But it was special. Wink! Wink!

The job of a crewperson is precisely the same on these sets as on any set. The crewmembers get the set ready for filming the "Talent" (aka the actors—only these actors had different talents, let's say). This new crew member was like a kid in a candy store, holding the Golden Ticket. He knew he would probably burn in hell but like a moth drawn to the light…

First time on a movie set! (Guaranteed true!)

For ease of conversation, like a movie, let's start at the beginning… my beginning. On my first day on an actual movie set, I thought I had died and went straight to heaven. I arrived just before breakfast time. They had a huge… and I mean a massive spread of food. Best of all, it was all free for the crew. (Free… who gives away free food… three times a day?) Well, anyway, they had lox and bagels. (I later discovered lox was nothing more than salmon cured in salt. Hey, I grew up in Inglewood, CA.) They had eggs Benedict, or they would make you a breakfast burrito on request. They had a cook ready to take your order. I had him make me an omelet I would have paid big bucks for in a restaurant. There was not even a tip jar. I put everything expensive on that omelet. He just smiled and made it quickly. I found myself hovering like a vulture, waiting until he finished. He then placed some home-fried potatoes beside it and handed me the plate. I must tell you; I believe it was just pure delight. Afterward, hanging around the breakfast table with a few of the guys I had been introduced to, they said it was time to go to work. I swallowed almost all my food quickly.

Now ready for action. My new life as a grip began shortly. Like most things, it took me a little while to get the hang of gripping. Finally, I worked my way up the pecking order of callbacks. The critical grip has a list of people he calls first, second, third, and fourth. I was about his twenty-fifth call. I think the Town was so busy that he just got down to the ""U"s" on his list. I soon found that other Key grips wanted me for my services. That's a pretty good feeling. Then, I landed a great job as a grip driver. You would drive the truck full of motion picture equipment to the location. This truck was called the grip truck. It contained all the grip equipment needed for the day's shooting schedule. I would always start work, usually an hour before everyone else's call time – the time to report to set – ready to work. Then, I would work alongside all the grips all day long. After a reload of the truck, I'd take it to a gas station and refuel it and the generator. The beauty of this job was I was on the time clock. I was making the big bucks. HUGE money! Then came the wine and song. I was like a puppy, rolling over and over in a grassy field. My life was in perfect working order.

How I explain the working of a movie set

I am often asked how to explain the working atmosphere on a movie set? So, I explain to people using a few different movies. These films are close to being on a lot of working sets. After you watch some of the films below, you will have a general feel of how it really is. Albeit not perfect, it is damn close to how it is! Here they are in alphabetical order:

A Cock and Bull Story.

And God Spoke!

Babylon!

Day for Night.

Living in oblivion.

Once upon a Time in Hollywood.

State & Main.

The Offer.

The Player.

Tootsie.

Tropic Thunder.

These movies should and might give you some idea of authentic controlled chaos that (sometimes… well, most times) goes on behind the scenes. Basically, in some respects, they all resemble a Film Life documentary of sorts.

Questions I always get! (Guaranteed true!)

*Are some of the big-name star's idiots as reported?

Answer: Yes, there are a few jerks. It could be .005 percent——a tiny fraction, especially compared to most other types of work. (But that is my impression.)

*Are there overnight sensations?

Answer: I have seen ordinary people pulled out of a crowd and get their SAG cards. (Me included.)

*Can you tell us what your favorite things that you have done that most people may not believe?

Answer: I have over forty years of favorite things, but the Lone Ranger was my OMG moment. As I took a photo standing next to Clayton Moore (The TV Lone Ranger), I felt like a seven-year-old boy again. Thrilled… excited… and delighted with boyish sloped-in shoulders and a Cheshire cat smile! I will never forget that moment! This was followed up by a photo with astronaut Buzz Aldrin! A true American hero in my eyes.

*Do you have to have a college degree to make it in the film industry?

Answer: Absolutely… not! I did not even finish high school in the late sixties. (Not bragging.)

*How do you get on a film shoot in the first place?

Answer: Nepotism! My sister was dating a guy who was working as a grip on nonunion commercials.

*How would someone who doesn't know anybody in Hollywood get a job making movies, videos, or documentaries?

Answer: Learn… everything you can about the movie-making industry. The more you know, the faster you grow! There is lots of stuff on YouTube. (Not all is true, but if you hear it repeated in different videos, chances are, there is a nugget of truth there.)

*Is it all as glamorous as it appears to be?

Answer: Yes, and then some. To this day, I cannot believe that I have traveled to many parts of the world, stayed in four—and five-star hotels, and dined with so many great artists. I indeed developed imposter syndrome in the beginning. But then you grow into your craft. (But I still fake it a lot of times… in conversations.) So, sue me!

*Is it all made up, or is it true?

Answer: It is indeed made up to look true in a most imaginary way! (Welcome to Hollywood!)

*What happens on a film shoot?

Answer: Everything, nothing, all at once? You plan, follow a plan, and you go home after the plan. The only thing is… usually, it's lots of fun doing so… well, most of the time. I liken it to living at Disneyland. It's natural, but it is not! Yet, it is the best place on earth. (Put the paid "Disney" Product Placement Advertisement here!) (Side hustle… you'll see.)

*What are the stars like on the set?

Answer: The good ones have done their homework, arrived in plenty of time knowing their lines, and turned out an adorable product.

*What is the craziest thing you've ever done in Hollywood?

Answer: Put Horse droppings in the trunks of the Advertising Agency executives! No wait… there was this one time…

*What is the worst thing you've ever done in Hollywood?

Answer: If I remember correctly, I crawled very close to a giant moving turning wheel on the sky cable gondola in Jackson Hole, Wyoming, while it was rotating to attach a pulley system to the superstructure. I earned the DFC (Dumb Fu*k Certificate) Award for that move. (It was not my most brilliant move.)

*What kind of money can you make working in Hollywood?

Answer: It depends on what position you end up in. As a working crew person, I usually earn between $60K and $120K, strictly on average, currently. I have earned far less and far more. (If the IRS is reading this, I have reported every dime…and some nickels, too.)

*What secrets can you tell us about what happens behind the scenes in Hollywood?

Answer: Easy answer; turn some more pages and enjoy.

*What the hell is a grip?

Answer: I was once told by a great cameraperson that a grip is – intelligent muscle. (I somewhat agree with that amusing statement.)

Place Joke here:

Hey, what do most crewmembers call those things that you blow and make a wish?

Answer: Breathalyzers!

What you see and what you don't repeat. (Guaranteed true!)

It's like that Las Vegas mantra: What goes on in Vegas stays in Vegas! Believe me, it is incredibly accurate here. I have seen it, heard about it, or did it myself! (Well, not everything!) I'm not bragging; I was just at the wrong place and time. I will take most of it to my grave… but here are some more tasty morsels before I go! Bon appétit! (or as they say in the film, "Lunch - One Hour!") You'll see what I mean.

Are these stories real?

I can vouch for most of these stories. As I said, I participated in "a lot" of the book's contents. The others have either been first person heard, personally seen, or I have seen photos. Believe me, you can bet your bottom dollar there are many cans of kernels of truth spread throughout this book. While the other is strictly B.S.!... or is it? (I don't want any lawsuits here!)

(Hey, I know that guy!)

(A young Santa Claus in the makings)

Oh, before you, there was someone else in this business. After you, there will be someone else! (Ego problem solved)

The film business is about professionalism, loyalty, and a strong work ethic. If need be, you can learn to fake all three until you can make it.

If you are making a film, "Never spend your own money."

If you are not busy, stay out of sight!

If you tell the truth, you don't have to remember what you said! (Mark Twain)

If you're not just appearing, you're most likely disappearing.

If you're unsure, shoot with a wide lens... you're bound to film something interesting!

Regarding the film industry, "Nobody knows anything while everyone knows everything."

It is whispered that Ricky Gervais said, don't worry, nobody else knows what they're doing either.

Keep your shoes shined. (It is noticed.) I have been told on many occasions that you always have shined shoes. (I wear Ecco Chukka-half boots a lot!) My answer always is that I was a former Marine for 8 years. Now that they know a bit of my history, they will most likely decide about me.

Leave a daily tip for housekeeping at the hotel. (Different daily housekeepers)

My "Ace in the hole" is under-promise, then over-deliver. (You'll be back; I promise you that!)

Never trust a fart!

One Rule

As a film crew member, you can be anything in film production but must be on time.

Please and thank you go a long way.

Remember, the product might be the most useless object ever invented, but if you polish it and make it sparkle, some sucker will always buy it!

Whatever advice you have received about the film industry, someone else will tell you the opposite.

Show up. Pay attention. Keep your sense of humor.

Tell the truth. Admit mistakes and move on.

The key to a comfortable retirement is paying for your home.

Walk with purpose.

You most likely will NOT wish you had worked one more production day on your deathbed.

You're only as good as the crewmembers that you work with!

Your poor planning is not my emergency.

Heard on Set

Are you helping me, or are you F-ing me, because you're sure as hell not F-ing helping me now!

The A. D. said to his P.A., There's no I in… Hey, F-you, I'm your boss!

An alternative statement could have been, keep it up, and there'll be no "u" in tomorrow.

An inexperienced Director asked, can you make it brighter? An answer came back quickly. I've got so much F-'ing light in here, I could weld with it.

Hollywood proverb: The work will persistently expand to the time allotted.

Are you a saboteur or part of my paid crew?

If you don't like this speed, you'll hate my other one.

Are we going to film it or paint it? I get paid by the hour either way.

Well, we fooled them again. (Said often at wrap time.)

Keeping you is like sending two good workers' home.

The same person always seems to call out, 10-2, right after we get back from lunch. This person's mantra was, the boss makes a dollar, I make a dime. That is why I dump on company time.

Hair, corn, and peanuts. When someone asked what that meant, they answered that those are the only three things that come out the same way they went in; the rest are usually fixed in post.

Heard on set: We don't have time to reload.

An annoying UPM complained when told that they needed a huge, expensive light to illuminate the Union train station windows in L.A., Saying, I've never lit Union Station this way! The gaffer replied, I've seen your IMDB; you've never lit anything.

Stories Spread Around Town (Almost Guaranteed True!)

In the eighties, a film called By Night was directed by Mr. Robert McCall (not his real name). This crew member met the actors and actresses in the morning just before they began a rehearsal. Oh, s--t! Never had this film person seen rehearsing like that! Before that first day, the worst he had ever viewed was a Playboy or a raunchy, dirty magazine. It was now Columbus, sailing into a whole new world. After work, the cast and crew went to a local bar. The key grip, Reginald (not his real name) tried to pull a fast one on the new guy. He had the lead actress, Veronica (not her real name), put the moves on the newbie. Surprisingly, the targeted person held his own. He let her go through her sexist spiel, and when she finished, he said, "Okay, thanks. Hey, where did you come from?" It was like a light switch had flipped off inside of her.

She went from hooker mode to poor country girl. She had a lot to say to someone – anyone that would listen. She basically spilled her life story that Night. The targeted person was moved by her. He felt like two people were living inside of one woman's body.

The next day, there were more scenes to be shot. They were tame by today's standards. Hell, you have probably seen worse on streaming T.V. By the time the sixth and last porno came around, the young colt was ready for the pasture. He was done. He had seen it all. He had just worked with the world-famous Johnny H. (Lord, that guy would make a horse blush.) That was it; this was his last special.

Besides, he had been lucky to not get arrested for stealing shots. (Stealing shots is where you film in an area without a film permit.) It's not like you can call City Hall and say, "Hey, we're filming an illegal porno in your fair city, and we want to have a legal permit. Oh yeah, we're going to show the Golden Gate, and oh yeah, we're going to film a sex act in front of the local police station with John H." Fat chance. They had filmed right in front of the police station. His nerves could not take it. After finishing the flick, he told the producers, "Don't call me again. If we pass on the street, you don't know me; I surely don't know you." He was paid for his services, which was the end. Or so he thought. Three days later, after a small stress-free sight-seeing of San Francisco, the filmmaker flew back to Los Angeles that following Friday.

On Sunday, he wanted to do something nice for a girl he was seeing. On the way to her home, he stopped at a nice-looking flower shop in the local mall. Behind the counter was a young woman who owned the quaint little, high-end store. She was dressed very… very conservatively, with her hair up in a schoolteacher-style bun. One customer was paying for their flowers, and a few were shopping. The hurried movie maker asked, "Excuse me, miss."

As she looked at him, her face drained white. He is sure that he saw her lips quivered. She squeaked, "Uh... may I... may I help you, sir?" Her eyes darted to her other unaware customers. Then they turned back to the young man, her eyes pleading silently.

He said, "Yes, ma'am. May I have a single red rose with Baby's Breath, please?" Baby's breath is that tiny white flower sometimes wrapped with the central flowers. It decorates the rose. Oh yeah, did I happen to mention the lady who owned the shop was one of the actresses, the porn star he had just finished working with several days prior? After that day, the movie maker decided to buy his future flowers… elsewhere. This would benefit his nerves and the shop owner's blood pressure.

Pacino (Guaranteed accurate!)

Years ago, I was filming a commercial at Raleigh Studios across the street from Paramount Studios. One day, I wrapped a little early, around 5:30 p.m. This is a rarity in the film world. It was still daylight, something we rarely see at the end of the workday. I was driving off on my brand-new, shiny Harley-Davidson motorcycle. I had put a lot of extra chrome on it, and it looked nice if I do say so myself. I paid about $17,500.00 for this sleek, mean motorcycle machine. It was the Classic model, the one with the smaller front wheel.

As I was slowly working through all the cars in the parking lot, a crew of big production trucks was slowly pulling into place. This slowed down my exiting process. As I waited patiently, a man in a cook's outfit, wearing a scarf, walked by me. He stopped to look at my motorcycle. "Nice bike," he said.

I turned to him and saw a pair of bright brown eyes with a great smile. The cook had spilled something on his white tee shirt. His apron was a little soiled around his waist. I believed him to be one of the workers at our studio's restaurant cantina. It was located a few doors down from the stage I was leaving. He looked familiar, so I guessed he was either a busboy or a cleanup cook. He asked me how I liked my Harley. My reply was, "It's the best thing I've ever had between my legs."

He smiled and asked, "Did it cost very much?" "Yes, they can be a bit pricey, but if you really want one, they have financing," I told him that I had only put $500.00 down and was financing the rest. He smiled and said thank you as he walked off towards stage 12.

I remember thinking, I don't know what a cook's wages are, but if he had enough money to put down, he could buy one himself with the right financing. I hoped for the best for the guy and took off towards home.

About eleven months later, I was watching a brand-new movie starring Michelle Pfeiffer and Al Pacino. As I watched, my mouth fell open. They cut to a scene in which Al Pacino played a cook behind the counter, trying to pick up on the waitress, Michelle Pfeiffer. The movie was called Frankie and Johnny! He had been the cook I met in the parking lot on that day of my slow exit.

Years later, I worked a few days on a movie, Heat, starring Mr. Pacino. I was too afraid and embarrassed to ask him if he remembered when he met a rider on a shiny new Harley-Davidson at Raleigh Studios.

(This is not one of those Hollywood fairytales I told you about. I have no way to prove what I just told you, but I find it funny today.) Hey, I may ask him someday!

I'm Not Dead! (Guaranteed true!)

A commercial with a mammoth director was a six-week Chevy commercial. We started our first day of filming in Chicago. We were being put up at the Ritz Carlton Hotel, the fanciest hotel I had ever stayed in.

The production company paid for the room. All I had to pay for was incidentals: meals in the room or anything from the overstuffed bar. They had soda, booze, and exotic candy. Every Night after work, I would have a different type of chocolate bar from several countries. They were great. They were also ten bucks apiece! I was surprised to find out how much they cost. I found out the day I checked out. Who knew the Ritz would charge so much for a simple candy bar? Other than that, the hotel was beyond fantastic.

One day, we went on a city scout and returned to the hotel for a late lunch. I had never been on a big-money commercial before, so when the bill came after they had lunch and a few bottles of wine, I figured I had to chip in. There were only ten people—how much could it be for a game hen and a few bottles of wine?

Holy s---! I got a glimpse of the bill. It was one thousand-two-hundred-thirty-six dollars before the tip! My hand slowly moved away from my wallet area. Who the hell pays over a grand for lunch? It was the Director, the producer, the production manager, the art director, a gaffer, four high-priced agency people, and me. Welcome to the big show, kid. (To reiterate, I was born in Inglewood, CA. We were so poor that I could not even pay attention.)

The next day after the scout, we had lunch at the Ritz again, plus two more bottles of wine. What was the tab on that? At that point in my life and career, I fully remembered what my father said:

"Mike, keep your mouth shut and your ears open. Learn to smile and nod a lot." My father spoke wise words.

The Chevy spot was to be six weeks long but was extended two weeks after the clients saw the footage. I was informed that they tossed another million into the mix. It was initially budgeted for just under two million. Then, the agency added another state they wanted to work in: Hawaii! After we finished Chicago, Northern California, and San Diego, we would travel to Hawaii for two weeks.

My only concern besides the $750 a day I was earning was finding a good crew in the different locations. The crews are great worldwide, but you don't get the "A" team workers if the Town is busy. In Chicago, they were making a movie called "The Untouchables" at the same time, starring Kevin Costner and Sean Connery. The stars were staying at the same Ritz as well. I found this out the hard way.

On the first day of the shoot, José, my best boy, had flown in the Night before. As we were riding down in the Ritz's crowded elevator. I was complaining about how all the excellent crew had been sucked up by the "Untouchables' film crew, and we could only get the "B" or "C" crewmembers (not as experienced).

José said he knew, but big stars like Costner and Connery drew long workloads.

I told José, "Sean Connery, that old guy – I thought he was dead."

Near the elevator door, as they were opening to let off its human cargo, I heard a Scottish voice say, "I'm not dead!"

All I could see through the disappearing crowd was the back of the living Mr. Sean Connery (so sorry, sir!). At that moment, I thanked God that I was short. (BTW, Jose is alive and can prove what I said is true.)

Priceless Crystal Chandelier

Over the years, I have traveled to many locations. Some were everyday places, some were historic, and some were priceless. This one was priceless. The film was shot deep in the state of Louisiana. My crew of Merry Grips and I were filming on a plantation built before the Civil War. It had high ceilings, hardwood floors, and a six-foot by eight-foot crystal chandelier. This lamp had been shipped from England and was much older than the mansion.

It had been lovingly cared for through the past few centuries. Now, a crew would film at this splendid location and capture images to show the world its abundant beauty.

The rehearsal was completed with the actors. All that was required now was setting up a few more lights to enhance the three-hundred-year-old crystal lamp. They would reflect the light like hundreds of dangling prisms. All the movie lights were set except for the last one. It had to be placed high on a ledge to backlight the scene. A ten-foot ladder was called for over the radio.

"I've got it," the voice of an eager young grip named Troy called out from the over-filled motion picture equipment truck. In a moment, Troy, with the ten-foot ladder perched on his right shoulder, raced in excitedly to the waiting hands of the key grip... me! Then, as if in slow motion before the crew's eyes and mine, a mighty freight train, a bull in a China shop, and Captain Chandelier – all in one – decided to race in. With the long ladder perched high on his shoulder, the front end raised so as not to hit anyone. But not low enough to avoid hitting something... say… priceless.

The once still majestic crystals helplessly fell like blades of clipped grass. No! Troy! It was too late! The chandelier was trimmed down the middle like a reverse Mohawk. Holy crap! My life, like the smashing crystals, flashed before my eyes.

What to do? What to do? It was 10:30 p.m. People were tired, and this was the last scene for the Night. It was the very last shooting day at that historic location before we packed the trucks to travel some sixty miles away from the scene of the crystal crime caper to the city's next-day location.

I made a command decision. It was someone in my department (who was now nicknamed "Chandelier") that had caused the damage. It was my grip that destroyed the timeless work of art in glass. I had to find courage and step up to the plate. I grabbed the ten-foot ladder from Troy before he could swing it around, causing further damage. I looked at my grips, and they looked back at me. It was settled! I hurried up the ladder. The grips gathered the evidence – the chipped and cracked crystals – and quickly handed them to me individually. I re-hung them in under two minutes flat. I tell you; we looked like a NASCAR pit crew. I mixed in the now somewhat shortened glass, re-posting good ones that hung higher to a lower perch. When it was finished, it "almost" looked correct.

The actors and the Director returned to the set when we said, "We're ready!" Everyone returned, and the scene was quickly shot. No one noticed the "new and less improved" chandelier. We packed up that Night and traveled like a band of gypsies. (Can I say that?) After that, "Chandelier" (i.e., Troy) could only carry a four-foot ladder. No higher than his eyebrows. I do not believe anyone knows except for the grips… and God!

Cajun Country

I became an honorary Cajun. (Of course, they used a different term.) One for a person of Cajun ethnicity. Some view it as derogatory. However, many Cajuns embraced the name.

I later found out after I was bestowed this honor. It means you're a good person in a Cajun's book. You will be treated like family, and you'd better learn to like spicy food. Me, I wouldn't say I like anything spicier than ketchup. But you don't, and you can't turn down these salt-of-the-earth people. If they were a family of ten, you'd make #11, and even if there's only one skinny chicken for dinner, I am sure you'll get an equal share.

Here's how I entered this distinguished membership of esteemed Cajuns. I was working on a movie called "Man Hunter" for Cannon Films. Its' star was Michael Dudikoff. I had hired about five local personnel from Homa, Louisiana. They knew the swamps well. I needed these men to build "underwater walkways" and satellite landing platforms (Used for the light stands) for the movie.

The local men brought chainsaws to work in the swamps to cut down stumps, called Cypress Knees, that grow out of the water. The platforms needed to be underwater about 6 inches. The men would then lay in plywood and nail it to the underwater flattened stump. This way, the actors could run through the swamp, fight, and roll around. Actors would have been bogged down in the mud if these platforms had not been built. We used about 187 sheets of four-foot by eight-foot, three-quarter-inch thick, construction-grade, C/D plywood.

A sign quickly went up in my honor, "Uva City. "We filmed there for three weeks. On the last day of filming, one of my local (Cajun) grips came to me and asked, "Hey Sher, what's y'all going to do with that plywood when you're done making your movie?"

"Toss it," I said. "Why? Do you want it?" It had been underwater for over three weeks now.

"Why Sher, we take it land yap (free), if you don't mind."

"But it's wet, probably warped," I said.

"Sher, it'll dry, be good as new, he replied. Probably going to build us another bedroom."

Then, an idea came to me immediately. "Wait right here," I told him.

I left to talk to the producer. I knew the producers would say, "Yes, no problem." But I wanted to get my hard-working men a kiss (a bonus.)

"Bill," I said to the producer, "we have got to trash out all that water-damaged plywood tomorrow when we are finished shooting. I told my guys I might be able to get production to pay them $100 to $150 cash each to carry it out this coming Saturday. They told me they would haul it away for me for free."

Bill immediately jumped on the $100 value. (As I knew that he would) "Good. I'll pay them $100 each, but they have got to haul it all out by Saturday night."

Don't you ever worry, I thought to myself. When I told my foreman (lead Cajun) that the producer would only "pay them" a hundred dollars each but that they must "haul it ALL away," a big old toothy grin crossed his weathered face. He said, "Sher, when you first came here from Hollywood, I didn't like you folks much. But you, Mike, are a good man! So, Y'all are now a c#@n-ass. You be coming Saturday night to my house for supper."

The compliment was worth a million to me. Dinner was wonderfully delicious, even though I still do not have any stomach lining left from the spicy food. What an incredible honor and memory. (I have photos)

Gator Moving

I went down to Florida with José to film a Toyota truck commercial. The concept was that three pals were helping a buddy move using his brand-new crew cab truck, which would seat five souls. The "gag" in the commercial was that the men were driving a giant alligator in the truck's bed. They loaded the gator into the truck bed, tail first. Near the cab, two heavy ropes on each side were tied to the gator's neck, preventing the gator from crawling out the back of the truck. The men jumped into the three-door cab and drove off on the thick tree-lined road in the heavy swamp area.

This worked flawlessly twice. However, on the third take, after the men securely clipped the gator in, they jumped into the cab and began to drive slowly down the dirt road. Suddenly, all the doors rapidly opened. All the men jumped from the still, slow-moving vehicle. The gator figured out he could not exit the back of the truck bed, but it didn't stop him from turning and smashing through the back window. See you later, alligator.

Baby Gator Paralyzing Saliva

This job was a lot of fun for José and me. This is where we acquired a reputation as practical jokesters and highly professional liars.

We had been working on this alligator farm on this same truck commercial. The "gator farm" raised the gators from birth. There were babies, one month through 12 months old. The gators were in big metal tubs. It was exciting to see so many. We all posed and took pictures near the tubs. Mike, the advertising agency head guy, wanted a photo as well. We had him hold a two-foot-long gator by the tail. He smiled for the camera.

Just as we snapped the photo, the baby gator used its tail strength, turned on his tail, and "nipped" Mike's hand on the fingertip. The picture was priceless. This is where our practical joke began. I asked Mike if he had been hurt by the tiny bite. (It was just a scratch!) He replied, "No."

José jumped in and said, "Good thing he didn't break the skin." Mike looked puzzled at José. José explained, "These are just baby alligators. No real strength in the jaws yet. So, much like a baby rattlesnake with poison, they are born with a paralyzing venom in their saliva. This way, they break the skin of their prey and hold on tight, like the big gators. The saliva will enter through the puncture marks and slow down the heart." Then he added, "Sort of makes the pray sleepy." He finished with, "Good thing. See ya," as he walked off. The seed had now been planted.

Mike looked at me to see if what José had said was valid. I just yawned wide (making Mike yawn) and pretended like I was hearing something in my microphone earpiece. I answered, "Okay, boss. I'm on it," as I ran off waving goodbye without giving him an answer.

About an hour passed as José and I set up the next shot. We noticed that Mike, the head of the advertising agency, was missing. That is no problem. We will just follow the shooting schedule. About five hours passed before we saw him again. In the distance, we heard Mike's voice yelling, "Where the hell are José and Mike?" We both ran and hid until he cooled down and told the other agency reps of his trip to the emergency clinic.

Mike was concerned about the skin breaking. He started feeling a little tired, not to mention that we had already worked about 50 hours in four days, plus the hour-and-a-half drive from town to location. Hell, I was tired also!

After Mike's third yawn and checking his fingers several times, he felt it prudent to get his medical wounds checked out. He had a production assistant (P.A.) drive him back to town to the hospital to have his finger looked at. The doctor swabbed his scratch with alcohol on a Q-tip and put a Band-Aid around it.

Mike was puzzled, so he asked the doctor, "What about the paralyzing poison?"

"What poison?" the doctor replied, followed by "it may have bacteria, but no poison."

"You could have seen the turkey feathers growing on him as his face turned red," I was told by the P.A. He raced the one-and-a-half hour back in hot pursuit of José and me! After that, the word was out on the two tricksters: "Watch out for José and Mike!" (We had now become infamous in Hollywood!)

Missed the Bus

On another commercial in Knoxville, Tennessee, the head electrician (Jeff B.) and key grip Gerald U. set each other off. Jeff did not like him much in the first place, and he did not like Jeff B. either. Both professionals knew it would only be three grueling days of work. They could both tough it out.

This situation taught me that the best revenge is served rather coldly. Finally, it was the last day of filming, so when the crew wrapped up, just like magic, all was forgiven... for now.

Off to the bar at the hotel the crew went. There were slaps on the back – "you're the best crew I have ever worked with" was on its repeating loop. Smiles all around. It felt like the crew was on "Fantasy Island."

As Gerald U. stumbled to his room from the bar, knowing that they were leaving in a few hours (at 6:00 a.m.) Gerald spotted the hotel's courtesy house phone. He just had to do it. He picked up the handset, ringing the front desk's phone immediately.

"Front desk," a voice emitted.

You're up, Gerald, thought to himself. "Hello, this is Jeff B. I want to change my wake-up call to sleep in, say, 9:00 a.m."

"You're all set, Mr. B. I have changed it from 5:00 a.m. to 9:00 a.m. Have a good night's sleep."

Click. The phone went dead. I'm dead if I get caught, Gerald thought. He chuckled, shrugged his shoulders, and then shuffled to his room.

The following day, at 6:00 A.M. sharp, the entire crew sat in the shuttle van waiting to travel to the airport. It seemed only one member was not in the vehicle. The First AD cried out, "Has anybody seen Jeff?"

Gerald sat in the van, quiet as a field mouse. The unit production manager called, "Okay, drive around back to his room and knock on the door." Knock-knock. No answer. Knock, knock, knock. Harder. Nothing! As the First AD turned to leave, the door cracked open. An unshaven, disheveled Jeff stood there groggily. His eyes grew as he noticed the entire crew in a van waiting.

"We're leaving in two minutes," the Unit Production Manager screamed. Get in the van or catch a cab." Within a minute and 12 seconds, Jeff was out his door. His suitcase still had a shirt sleeve or two hanging out. There was no time to comb his hair, brush his teeth, or shave. I must tell you, he looked like "hammered shit."

Gerald, on the other hand, felt like a million dollars. (It must have been his four hours of sleep.) Cold duck, anyone?

Squat in the field!

I was given a job to travel to North Carolina (Raleigh area) to film an Army Reserve commercial. I was thrilled to go. Once there, I could fly in a Black Hawk helicopter, ride inside an armored transport, and mount a Panavision camera on the barrel of a MIA1-Abrams 67-ton tank. The Army wanted to show the prospective Army Reserves all the machines they could operate.

First, we filmed a 105mm cannon shooting off several rounds. The recoil and blast were something I cannot describe. Then we filmed a "pretend" strike zone next to a bridge on flat ground about 100 feet off the road. The Army Reserve explorative ordinance officer told his men to go in and plant explosive charges to be filmed for the reenactment. I built an open-back three-wall bunker/revetment out of three-quarter-inch construction plywood. The front plywood facing the explosion had an 8"x8" hole cut through it. On the front face of the plywood, I placed a three-quarter-inch thick by 1'x1' piece of bulletproof Lexan – an optically clear plastic sheet. The two-sided sheets of plywood were positioned at 45° angles to redirect any concussion or debris. This was all braced off by 2'x4' and 4'x4' lumber.

This was overbuilding for the protection of the camera. I had never seen firsthand what an explosive charge would and can do. Besides, we were only filming the effect of an explosion. The Army Reserve guys saw things differently; I was to find out.

"All set" was called out. All personnel not directly related to the filming backed up the road one-half mile. "One-half mile," I thought. It's just a movie—a commercial. Okay, better to be safe.

We moved back. An armored troop carrier was brought in so the cameraman and assistant could duck into and flip the remote cable on/off switch. Once everyone was safely in place, "Going hot" was called out. The explosives were now ready for the button to be pushed. "Roll camera" and "speed" (which means the camera is running at the proper speed of 24 frames per second) were yelled.

"Fire!" Ba-boom! The motor home, which I was standing behind one-half mile away, shook hard. "What the hell?" I ducked instinctively. The explosion was massive. We all began to wonder if there was a problem. A few minutes later, an all-clear call was sounded.

It was still solid when I returned to my revetment (the plywood shield). I smiled. But there was a problem. The concussion from the explosion was so significant that it wrapped around my structure and squeezed the camera magazine. This compartment feeds the film to the camera. We had captured the explosion only to the point of the initial blast before it snapped the film.

After that, I walked over to the area where the road was. There was now a thirty-foot wide, eight-foot-deep crater. All I could think about after seeing the massive hole was a line from the movie "Butch Cassidy & The Sundance Kid": Sundance turns to Butch after he blows the money safe to smithereens, "Use enough dynamite there, Butch?"

This same commercial had a few other noteworthy things happen while filming it. About an hour after the explosion sequence, I strolled to a nearby field. A sudden urge to go #2 hit me. I was about five hundred yards from the motor home. I did not think I would make it back in time, so I went freestyle, just like our founding fathers did hundreds of years earlier. I found a suitable location in some thick, tall grass and squatted down to do my business.

As I cared for my needs, I felt tall grass tickling "the boys" down there. Then, the tall grass started crawling up Mount Rushmore and his adjoining friend. It was the most significant bug I had ever seen, looking me straight in the eye. I smacked it hard. Boohoo! That hurt! I fell back, missing my… offerings by an inch.

I scooted forwards like a dog rubbing his butt on the grass. No more bugs! Luckily for me, I was carrying my drinking water bottle. I cleaned up in the wilderness and have for the first time ever just shared this story with people. (Please, don't tell anyone else… ever!

The Tool Bag Is Full of Chicken!

I would travel around the United States and hire local grips during my movie career. The grips I got, where I went, were pretty good. I hire people by attitude as well as abilities.

We were in Portland, Oregon. The local grip I hired was the reigning key grip in that area. Let's just call him "Ross" for legal purposes. Ross and I got along famously on the first day. By the second day of the four-day chicken shoot for Foster Farms, we were playing practical jokes on each other.

On the last day of the shoot, we shot on a local makeshift stage. I arrived in the morning, and my toolbox was hanging from the rafters. Ross walked in with a big smile on his face. I threw my hands in the air and told him, "Ok, you win," and I bowed to him. The day went on without incident. Ross kept an eagle eye on me, knowing that any moment now, I would return the favor in the form of a practical joke. I had the patience of Job.

We were setting up for the last shot, then we would wrap. I would finally travel back to Los Angeles. The cameraman, called for a piece of equipment. Since I was taking care of the dolly, Ross had to leave the stage to go to the grip truck, grab the equipment, and then run back in.

The truck was located right outside the door. He was not gone more than 15 seconds, thirty tops. I could only grab a handful of raw chicken and lift the tools in his grip tool bag sitting on the deck, about three feet from the Dolly. I threw the raw chicken into his tool bag, then threw the tools back on top.

Ross came back and quickly surveyed the area. I stood peacefully with both hands on the dolly control rod. We finished the last shot. I shook hands with Ross, walked him to his car, and told him what a great guy he was to work with. As he put his tool bag in the trunk of his car, I asked him when his next shoot days were. He told me about 10 days from that day. Work in Portland had been slow.

I smiled and vigorously shook his hand, saying, "Okay, pal, you'll hear from me. Or maybe I'll hear from you first?"

Three weeks passed after I returned home. One day, my wife, Sabrina, called me at work and told me she got a horrible, threatening message on the answering machine at home. When I got home, I listened to the message twice to thrice and started laughing out loud. I recognized Ross's voice immediately. All he could say was, "I'm going to kill you, you mother-F'er!

My wife wanted to know who I made so mad. I told her of the practical joke I had played on him. Old Ross did not actually have the last laugh. He had a ten-day-old rotting chicken accompanied by maggots in his tool bag. But the story does not end here. About two years later, as the legend of the rotting chicken grew in the film industry, a girl who had moved down to Hollywood from Oregon happened to tell my brother about the time a Los Angeles key grip came up to Portland and played a practical joke on the reigning key grip Ross, who was still located in Portland. My brother had now heard the other side of the story and could not contain his laughter. He introduced me to the girl and told her I was that bad LA key grip. We all laughed together.

The story continues. Many years had passed, and Ross had worked himself up in the ranks as a cameraman. He was assigned a job in the Los Angeles area near San Pedro, where I lived. My brother's good friend Steve had gotten a key grip job and hired my brother Rick as his best boy. Ricky instantly recognized Ross's last name. He called me and told me he was working close to my house. Ross was the cameraman on the shoot. Since I had last seen Ross, my brown curly hair had turned gray and a lot of it had fallen out. My waistline had increased exponentially.

My physical appearance showed that I had been living a pretty good life. There was no way that Ross or anybody else would recognize me now. So, I drove to the location where they were filming inside the gymnasium. They were shooting a non-union commercial in a union area. Ross was a non-union cameraman (leastwise, a Local 600 cameraman here in Hollywood).

I walked into the room in my cowboy boots, pressed pants, and wearing a dress shirt. I smiled at Rick, and he pointed toward Ross, who was setting up a shot with an NBA basketball player.

I walked up to Ross and said, "Hello, my name is Joey Belladouchie, I am the business agent for the Local 600 camera union here in Hollywood." Ross's face turned white. He picked up his camera and started scurrying across the basketball court for the commercial's producer. I was in hot pursuit. Knowing he had none, I asked him to see his Local 600 union card. I am so glad he did not slip and fall at the rate he crossed the floor. When he got to the other side, he introduced me to the producer as the business agent from the local union. He did not know what to do.

I reached out my hand and shook the producer's. "Hello. My name is Mike Uva, a local key grip in Hollywood, California."

The blood that had drained from Ross's face returned to make it flush. He was still hugging the camera, then put it down and looked at me straight. "You're Mike Uva?" he said. I started laughing along with my brother and Steve. We had a great laugh at poor Ross's expense. After Ross got over the initial shock of being scared out of his wit, he came around and laughed heartily with us. When I left that day, his parting words were, "You win; you are the King!"

It is good to be the king!

The Dummy!

If you've ever watched a Western movie, there are times when the wagon master says, "Circle the wagons." This was usually done at night, and the people would have a campfire in the middle.

The film industry's modern-day version is "circle the trucks." They would circle the trucks because we would be out on a location, either in the desert or the open plains, as the winds would come up. We could block the wind by circling the trucks and having a production camp. Hopefully, our tents would not fly away. The caterers would usually set up for this. They would cook their meals inside our open area.

One night, it was around 9:00 p.m. The crew had just broken for dinner. As we got our meals and sat down at our gusty, wind-blown tables, we heard the prop master yelling at his assistant. The prop assistant was sitting on the edge of one of the big motion picture trucks in a brown leather jacket. His black boots hung over the edge.

The prop guy yelled out, "Get off of the damn truck!" The prop assistant yelled, "The view is wonderful up here!" The prop master said, "Get off my F'ing truck now!" The prop assistant stood up and spoke, "Okay, I'm going to jump. Catch me!" The prop master yelled, "Don't jump – just climb down the other side."

The assistant yelled again, "I'm going to jump; I'm going to jump," as he backed away from the edge of the truck and out of sight. The prop master, now yelling louder, "Don't jump. You'll break your leg.

At this point, the entire camp seemed to watch the screaming match between the two people. Out of nowhere, we saw a body with a brown leather jacket and black boots fly off the top of the truck and crash onto a lone dinner table. The cast and crew were mortified. Then, they all howled out in laughter. Several people stood and clapped as they looked back at the prop truck roof. There stood the assistant. The entire crew had been set up by the two prop guys. They were compelling. This must have been a skit that they had done many times before.

You see, on top of the truck, out of the view of the entire cast and crew, was a dummy dressed exactly like the prop assistant who had been sitting on the edge of the truck. When he stood up, the assistant pulled back out of sight where nobody could see him, grabbed the dummy, and flung it as hard as he could. It landed on a table they had set up, causing it to crash to the ground.

We all looked at the prop assistant. He looked proud of himself as he stood there smiling. That was one of the best free shows I have ever seen.

José And the Toilet

José recently told me a story about himself. Both of us like a good practical joke. José's turn was up. He had been filming on location as an extra grip in a high-rise building in downtown LA. José excused himself so that he could relieve himself in the men's room down the hall. When he entered the room, it was an executive-style bathroom with fifteen private stalls. So, he went in, closed and latched the door, and began his business.

As he was sitting on the toilet, he heard his key grip boss and another man enter, talking to one another. José giggled to himself because he knew what he was about to do. As the guys were standing at the wall of urinals, José let out a small painful moan. Ooooooh!!! He heard his boss, and the other man giggle a little bit. José proceeded to let out a second, more extended moan. Oooooooooooh!!! The boss and the other man continued to laugh as they walked to wash their hands in the sink. This time, José let out one final cry.

"Help me," he screamed out in a low guttural tone. Both men ran out of the bathroom.

Gak - Yak - and the Lion!

Years back, I was working on a commercial for a kid's toy – a product called Gak. It reminded me of the toy Silly Putty from the '60s. It was a rubbery slime that was safe for kids to use – all nontoxic. This commercial had a farm theme with various farm animals: chickens, sheep, and a yak. The yak is a long-haired bovine (looks sort of like a buffalo in a long fur coat) from the

Himalayan region. These semi-trained yaks had been brought to the set by a very abled animal trainer.

In their inventory of animals, they brought a lion to the set. It was a young male, about two years old. He may have been young, but he was huge. I was allowed to take a picture with him outside of the stage. I was about 20 feet away as I was leaving when I stopped to speak to a friend. I turned back to look at the animal and made eye contact. He sprayed me. He positioned himself, then proceeded to mark his property from 20 feet. Everyone standing there laughed, of course, except me. But it was only a light mist, not a fluid stream, so it dried quickly.

My radio said, "Mike, we need you on set." I raced back in. The once peaceful set went nuts when I showed up. The yak, who was well settled, started rearing and trying to back away from where he was tied down. At first, I thought that I might have scared him by entering the set too fast. We are forever being told to move slowly around picture animals (trained ones). This yak would have no part of me. Then I realized what had happened. The smell of the lion was on me. The yak was not about to be lunch. The yak did not know that I, Michael G. Uva, was not much more than a cowardly lion. (I'm not lion-ing!)

Remarks Said on Movie Sets

If you're not going to work, get out of the way so I can.

Laughing our way to pizza.

A crewmember asked how we lost a whole crate of wood wedges? The response was one at a time.

Every day we work, we get a 1/2 day closer to the end of this movie.

The only thing you ever learn on a tech scout is where to park your car.

Big Time Director to crew: We can do these two ways, my way, or my way pissed off.

Big Time Director to crew: Great job, everybody. Nice try, DGA!

This is a great job; the only problem is that sometimes we must do it.

The work is easy; it's reading minds that so hard!

At breakfast, three more meals, and we are out of here.

The Six Steps in a Movie Production

1. Raring to go Enthusiasm.

2. Confusion.

3. Incompetence.

4. Terrorization of the Innocent.

5. Advancement of the Ineffectual.

6. Distributing the crew T-shirts.

Final Notice

A very well-loved English Grip, Mr. Vic Hammond (who was truly wonderful to work with), entered the producer's office and put his petrol bill on the producer's desk. The producer said: why are you showing me this? Vic's answered, because you've got my money, and they want to get paid.

Reasons Given to Quit High-Paying Crew Jobs!

I walked off a shoot because of the $5 a day that was due to me. When I am told something to my face and then blatantly renege on it. I just won't take it. Certain things piss me off. Number one is being lied to. I was popular enough to get another job quickly due to my good reputation. But never leave your crew short. So, I told the Key Grip, who I was working for, that after the week had finished. Production was changing locations and traveling to another state; I would not be traveling with them to finish the show. He understood why. Honesty matters to me.

On one show, the production company quietly dismissed the cops assigned to protect the crew to save on overtime money. This was all unbeknownst to the still-filming crew, who were filming in an evil, shady part of town loaded with lots of crime. Some of the crew picked up and left when they found out.

During the third week of shooting a low-budget movie, the production lied about the crew's paychecks; they said that the payroll company had screwed up. After someone called the always on-time payroll company, saying they had never received any money from the production company to pay the crew. The entire crew said, no money, no more honey! (work)

When safety and crew well-being are disregarded, it only takes a crewmember one day of shooting to see the production company's complete incompetence and extreme lack of safety protocols. That filmmaker did not return the second day.

An idiot crewmember lit a quarter stick of dynamite, thinking it might be funny.

You can only prepare enough for some of the different personalities you'll have to work with once you get to set.

My Story… What the Hell Is a Grip?

What the hell is a grip, someone asked! (I still get that question all the time.) The easy description is one a cameraman (David S.) once told me. His definition of a grip was "Intelligent muscle!" I like that. The grip, on most motion picture sets, is an expert handy person. Half engineer, half handy person. The cameraperson will have a right-hand person, commonly called the Gaffer. They are the head lighting technicians. The left-hand person for the cameraperson is usually called a Key Grip. The key grip is the HMFIC. He/She/them has a foreman of sorts, which is called a best boy/girl. The gaffer will also have a best boy/girl/them. (Regardless of whether the position is filled by a boy or girl, they're still considered the best boy on the call sheet. So much for political correctness there.)

After the best boy/girl, there are the workers—the grips. They will work the set. They also build scaffolding and mount cameras in the most precarious places to get that spectacular shot the director has dreamed up. They all work with a smile and never squeal, whine, grumble, or moan about anything. (Cut! Cut! Who am I trying to fool?)

My Own Boss – Way Back When…

After a few years in the film industry working as a non-union, free-lance grip, I landed a regular job as a 5-ton grip truck driver. The 5-ton grip truck looks like those large trucks you can rent from U-Haul or Penske moving rental services. Basically, it's a large moving truck that anyone can drive. (Under so many pounds, that is)

The grip 5-ton trucks are sometimes built a little longer with heavier wheels and transmissions. Underneath the big cargo box are several smaller boxes attached to the frame. The smaller additional boxes are called toolboxes or jockey boxes. These big 5-ton vehicles were designed to also pull portable generating units.

My life was now on track once again. I was clean and sober. I was driving about eighteen hours a day on average. I did this for about five years, and then one day, out of the blue, I got fired! The key grip that owned the grip truck I had driven exclusively for the past few years fired me on the spot off my next job.

Here is how it all went down. The essential grips truck had broken down a month before my release (Fired). The problem was that it was scheduled for a vast/high-paying, three-week commercial job in two days. The key grip would have to rent another truck from another grip company and hire their driver to do that job.

I was not about to lose three weeks of work! I had seen an older truck that had been up for sale for quite a while. It had been parked in Hollywood. I bought the beat-up truck because I knew it could do the job. I loaded all the equipment from his grip truck and did the job. He was paid quite handsomely for his equipment, and I was paid equally for my driving and griping services. When the next job came up, the key grip asked me, "What will you do with that truck?"

My answer was, I don't know, maybe I'll keep it! Wrong answer! I don't want the competition, he said. So, I've hired a permanent replacement driver for you, he informed me. He never gave me a chance. So, as you see, like the cliché goes, no good deed goes unpunished!

Shit, what do I do now? I had only one option! I would have to build my own grip truck. How hard could it be? I went to my local bank and applied for a loan of $20,000.

I sat with the loan officer and explained that I needed the money for motion picture grip equipment. Well, of course. A few questions were asked. What is grip equipment? Does it have a title or a pink slip? What is the default resale value worth? I said no to everything. The loan officer said, "I am afraid we'll just have to pass, but thank you for thinking of us." Try as I might, I could not get a bank loan… anywhere. The only thing left was to go to the loan sharks! (Did you know you can get hurt if you don't pay your bills on time with the Vig interest?) Okay, it wasn't a real loan shark, but it felt like one to me. Either way, I got the $20,000 I needed. Now on with the show… biz!

I had this old, secondhand, worn, and depleted 5-ton grip truck painted a glossy white. It was still an old truck, but it looked good now! I loaded it with all brand-new studio grip equipment. I have a heavily loaded, beat-up old truck that looks great! I sent out several snapshot pictures announcing a new kid in town. I would provide them with excellent service and new equipment! (Old truck – I didn't tell them that part! I guess it slipped my mind.)

After a few weeks, I received my first call. Hello, Uva's Grip Truck rental service, I answered.

Hi, I'm Joe from XYZ production company. We are filming a commercial this weekend, and I understand you're a key grip with a grip truck.

Oh, thank you so much for calling, but I am a grip truck driver with a fully loaded grip truck. But I am available for those shoot days, I replied.

I will call you back, replied to Joe. That bat rastard never called me back.

Another week passed! Ring, Ring. (Now polished somewhat.) Hello. This is Mike Uva with Uva's Grip Truck Rental Service. I answered.

Hi, this is Mary with Opic-Dopic Productions. I understand you are a key grip with a new grip truck package. My answer, why yes… yes, I am! My Key Grip career was started that very day. (Fool me once, shame on you. Fool me twice, shame on me.)

Years flew by and I found myself making money faster than ever. At the zenith of my business career, I had four full-size 5-ton grip trucks, three - three-ton camera trucks, and two 1-ton pickup trucks with six full-time employees. This is fitting for a high school dropout!

For me, becoming a grip seemed a natural and easy transition. I had a mechanical background and was trained by great grip teachers. What more could you ask? (Yes, I was a bit smug.)

Okay, now that I will become a big-time/full-time Key Grip, how will I learn all about it? Well, the internet hasn't been invented yet (as a matter of fact, I think we still have dial telephones). (Two tin cans and a string, if I remember clearly.) But once again, I digress. So, the next best thing was to go to the library and check out a book on gripping. When I arrived at my local library, I quickly discovered many books on the art of directing movies or how to become a cameraperson (PC). There was even a book on lighting a movie set. But there was not a single book on the art of gripping.

How was a young, non-union key grip supposed to learn the craft?

Easy. Just get into the union, and the other grips will teach you how to become a grip. But how do I get into the union? That's easy! You must be working on a motion picture. How do I get a job on a motion picture? That's easy! By being in the union. And so on… and so on… and so on.

I worked as a non-union grip for many… many… many years. By no fault of the unions, I just got fed up with trying to get in. I worked on as many jobs as possible. I learned as much as possible from the union grips, working on non-union shows when the union shows were slow, went on hiatus, or were nonexistent. I was very fortunate – I had been taught by some of the reigning key grips in the industry. (Leastwise, I held them in high regard.) I discovered along the way that a single piece of equipment had various names.

Example: There is a giant metal clothespin—the type you may have seen when a house is fumigated—and gigantic metal spring clamps. The giant clamps are sometimes called "number four," the next smaller ones are called "number three," the smaller hand sizes are "number two," and the smallest ones are—you guessed it— "number one."

But the story continues. This same clamp is also called a Hargrave and a Pony clamp and, lest we remember, a Brinks and Cotton. Oh! Did I also mention that it's also called a handy clamp? This was to name a few. I found out later that the four names were the manufacturers' company names: Hargrave, Pony, etc. This style of nickname reigned throughout most of the studio grip equipment. Then, they would have what they called East Coast gripping versus West Coast gripping. All very much the same, but different. And it's all very confusing.

I always carried a little notebook in my back pocket and a pen in my work pouch. This way, I could scribble down the names with a crude drawing (before phones with cameras) of each piece of equipment, so when I worked for different key grips and best boys, I knew what equipment they were talking about.

One year, I was on location in Louisiana, filming in downtown New Orleans. I was staying at the Iberville Hotel, overlooking the Mississippi River. In my mind, I had arrived. I was making what was considered a big buck picture.

The title was "The Big Easy," and the movie starred Dennis Quaid. (By the way, Dennis was fantastic to work with. Notice how I dropped the name Dennis as if he was my best pal/buddy. But Mr. Quaid is still a great guy!) It was a Sunday morning, and I was staring out the window while sitting at the desk provided in the room. I reviewed all my notes and papers, organizing them from A to Z. The stack had gotten quite thick. Being that close to God (on the 11th floor), I guess He struck my brain with a fantastic idea to write a book on gripping.

I told myself I would write it! It would become an overnight bestseller, and I would never have to carry another sandbag in my entire life. With this dream in place, I set out to work on the grip book.

Hollywood Cocaine Connection

I was now solid in the movie business; I had seen it all – or at least, I thought I had. I had seen some cast and crew members get shit-face drunk. In those days, every night after a long day of shooting, the production crew would break out a case or two of beer. (This used to be called wrap beer.) Productions no longer provide beer due to the legal liabilities, of course. Imagine your company supplying you with several beers after working twelve to eighteen hours daily? This is followed by the company saying, Goodnight, drive carefully! That just isn't going to happen!

After a beer or two, a few mellow members usually break out their vice of choice, which usually consists of Jack, Vodka, Grass, or Cocaine. It's funny—I was initially dead against getting loaded. Then I relented and asked myself, hey, what would one beer hurt? I did want to be sociable.

Then I reasoned, "What could one hit of grass do?" The worst thing that could happen – I would get a case of the munchies. Cocaine? Not me! No, not me! Not me, I protested!

Okay, just one toot! One snort! What could one little sniff of cocaine do to me? Yeah! This stuff was nothing.

I must have been waking up anyway. So, I'll try one more, free toot. Now I'm wide awake.

Then the question was asked, did I want to buy some for later? What is the cost? Okay, I'll take a quarter gram! Besides, $25 for a quarter gram wasn't that much money to me now. (Remember, only years before, I was earning $98 a month as a private in the Marines) And I was trying to be sociable. Now, for the strangest reason, I didn't seem as tired as before trying cocaine. I guess I must be getting used to the long hours of work.

I decided to get even more jobs now that I could work 24 to 36 hours straight. I would buy a $100 gram of cocaine as a pick-me-up. I wasn't hooked. Other people get caught. I was earning so much money now; what was $100? (Once a month's pay) I was making plenty of money. The weekend was coming up, and I was going out Saturday night. I had better get a little Coke for the weekend. I do not want to crash! Crap! Monday morning already? I had better get another gram to make it through the day. "So, what's a $100 a day?" I would make that much money in one hour and double the time.

This may sound embellishing, but I need something to prove to anyone! By my calculations, I probably put a Cadillac (at least a used Volkswagen) up my nose. (Granted, this was the '80s, and the cost of a Cadillac was a lot cheaper. A VW, much less.) Believe me, I am one of the lucky ones! Several crew members (now out of the movie business) put their houses up their noses, ruining their careers.

 I'm not standing on an apple box telling you the ills of drugs; it's just something I personally went through. It reminds me of when I was young, my father told me, Michael, fire is hot. The problem was that I had to learn for myself that the fire was, in fact, hot.

Drooling Laughter

Years ago, I worked on a Cheetos commercial with the great Jonathan Winters. He was a hilarious comic actor—pre-Robin Williams. Instead of demanding star treatment, Mr. Winters (Jonathan) would only sit with the crew at lunch. He was a regular, everyday guy—and funny as hell. The crew would be trying to eat their lunch as Jonathan went off telling his jokes.

We would laugh and smile and continue eating our meals. Jonathan would eat and continue his comedy. Within ten minutes, he had the entire table laughing so hard they were crying. They were holding their stomachs because they ached so severely with laughter.

I remember looking at the crew sitting at the table. They were paralyzed, frozen with laughter. A few grips were drooling. (Maybe they arrived that way.) Their mouths hung wide open, gasping for air, food still in them. If they moved, they might choke. It was as if Jonathan was the puppet master. He had a pleased look on his face.

So, Introduce Yourself

My career was blazing. I was traveling around the world doing various commercials from Argentina to Russia. I was just about to start feeling that "I had arrived." Wrong! I got a wake-up call and a reality check. I got embarrassed. (And I deserved it)

I was going to film a commercial on the beach in Malibu. Production figured we would only be needed for about four hours of shooting. Great – I could spend some quality time with my two kids. I had been traveling so much I hardly had time to sleep, let alone see my children. I was tired and stressed out. I discovered that I was yelling just a bit more and a little louder at my kids. But the next day, I would make it up to them… just after finishing my morning work. I would spend the rest of the day with Angela and David at Malibu Beach!

I had to wake my kids early to load them into the car for the early morning drive to Malibu from Valencia. They were groggy; I was tired and started yelling… once again. When I get mad at my kids, I would say rude things to "nudge" them back into line. This morning was no different. I was pissed. How the hell do your kids not understand what you want and what you need them to do? For God's sake – you're Uva's! Like the name "Uva" was noble or something. Better yet – don't tell anyone you're a Uva… I don't want to be embarrassed.

Finally, I got them settled in the car for a fun day at the beach. I woke them up an hour and a half later to tell them we had arrived. The sun should be up in about an hour. I'd be over at the grip truck across the parking lot if they needed me. So, I locked the car and went to work.

About five minutes after sunrise, I saw my two kids limping across the parking lot toward the catering truck where the crew had gathered for breakfast. I was sitting with this big-time commercial director, eating breakfast and schmoozing. When my kids arrived, the director stood up like a gentleman, reached his hand out toward my daughter, Angela, and introduced himself.

"Hi, I'm Peter S.," he said, knowing full well that these were my kids, "and you are?"

I smiled at how Peter treated Angela like a lady. Angela politely reached out her little hand and said, "Hi. I'm Angela."

Peter decided to take it further as he shook her hand. "Angela? Angela who?"

"Just Angela!" was her response. My smile melted. I was horrified.

Peter asked again, "Angela, don't you have a last name?"

"Nope!" Peter looked at me. I looked at Angela with daggers, then sheepishly looked back to Peter. Angela let me have the second shotgun shot to the gut. "My dad said, 'Don't tell anyone you're a Uva.'"

That was the coldest summer day at the beach in my life. Thank you, Angela…!

P.S. All is forgiven. You were right; I was wrong. I'm sorry. Love, Dad

My First Big Budget Key Grip Job

I had gotten a prominent feature (theatrical release) down in Louisiana as the key grip. José was my full-time best boy. Modesto, Bob, and Troy were the other grips to work the show with me.

This picture was going to be huge; I tell you. I read the script, and it was going to make it. I heard it even had a ten-million-dollar budget. That was the most significant movie I'd ever worked on as a key grip.

The crew and I arrived and started the picture. About a week in, my crew got tired of begging for a ride to go to the local hardware store some eight miles away from our shooting set on location, so José borrowed the producer's car for a quick run to the nearest store. (The producer got his vehicle back seven weeks later.) Every time the producer asked for his car, it seemed to be out on the run: getting equipment, getting hardware, going to the store, or whatever.

Have you ever seen a piece of plywood three quarters of an inch thick by 4' x 8' in size strapped to the top of a very expensive Cadillac? My crew even decided to decorate the car's interior. They hung the proverbial cotton dingle balls from the headliner, completely around the vehicle's inside. They also placed a ceramic dog in the back window. The head would shake as it drove down the street. I believe they call them bobbleheads.

Then, they really wanted the car to look cool, so they lowered the back end. Nowadays, kids call this slamming a car. The only way to lower that vehicle was to put about 450 pounds of sandbags in the trunk. But man, that car was excellent.

But our luck ran out on the seventh week. The boys (my crew) were following a substantial open truck carrying football-sized sugar beets nestled in their seats on the way to work. They wore head bandannas of various gang colors (the pink flamingos, the green tops, and the purple bad boys). Okay, it looked a little strange, but we never pissed any local gangs off.

The driver sat low in his seat. These guys were cruising. Even the 12-volt Christmas lights were working. They had been taped on the sides of the car. Wham! A colossal asteroid-sized sugar beet smashed out the front window, followed by three more sugar beets. Next was one headlight. Then, part of the car grill, followed by denting the hood. Finally, a sugar beet bounced and broke the front windshield out. It hit with so much force that it woke up two guys riding in the car. The driver hit the brakes hard, slamming all three grips forward, striking their head bandannas on the back of the seat.

"What the hell just happened?" I asked. "Who kicked out the front window?" And more importantly, "Who's going to tell the producer?"

So, we did the right thing… we went straight to the source—and—I lied! We took the car to the rental company, then we drove back to the hotel, turned in the nicest new clean car to the producer, and told him, "Thanks." Bewildered and befuddled, he never said a word. I think he was just happy to get his car back.

I don't think he even knew about the damage to the other vehicle until we wrapped (finished the movie.) And by that point, like most good crews, we were long… long gone.

The funny thing is that that producer never called me again to work on another film for him. (Maybe he just lost my telephone number.) Yeah, that's probably it. He just lost my telephone number.

After my return to Los Angeles, I went back to commercials. I didn't want to do another low-budget film. I really enjoyed making commercials more. They are faster-paced from the beginning to the end, and the pay is what we call above-scale. Then it happened. I hooked up with a crew of practical jokers when I went on location to shoot a commercial. And the gloves came off…

Watch What You Say!

Walkie-talkies are used every day in the film business. We all must use earphones or a headset. And no one wants a radio to go off during a film take, so we try to keep the chatter on the radio to a minimum. However, sometimes, some people don't know when to shut up.

One winter, during a night shoot on location, we were filming a scene of two people in a park sitting on a park bench in the evening. There were people strolling by in the moonlight in the background. We provided the moonlight. We will install a special bracket on a lift called a condor, a cherry picker, or a hydraulic arm with a safety railed basket.

It's like the type of phone or electric companies sometimes use. The arm is operated from inside the basket/bucket on the end of the arm. The operator rides the basket up into the air and adjusts the lighting unit, then sits in it for the duration of the scene. The condor operator usually brings something to sit on or a blanket, which is also quite common.

This operator also brought along his cell phone. During the middle of take #3, the arms boom operator was found to be in the middle of a personal phone call some sixty feet in the air. He had shifted his weight and leaned back against the railing, pressing the transmit key on his radio. It got stuck. His conversation was transmitted to everyone on his channel, including his boss.

Apparently, he did not like his boss. In fact, he hated him. The boss was a "jerk," an "asshole," and various other things he was heard saying. Unbeknownst to him, his boss heard every word.

After the movie scene was over and the boom arm was lowered, the operator's boss called him over to speak to him. The operator eagerly ran over and said, "Yes, sir? What can I do for you?" The boss asked, "Do you like your job?" "Yes, sir," was his answer.

"Good. Grab your tools and go to the production truck. The best boy will explain what he wants you to do next." I never saw Mr. Microphone again the rest of the night. Maybe he decided to go into broadcasting!

Rush to Russia

Man! It was cold in Moscow in November. I had landed a Pizza Hut commercial there. The star was to be Mr. Mikhail Gorbachev and his real granddaughter. (On YouTube – Pizza Hut – 1994 - Mikhail Gorbachev) While there, I had a first-hand, eye-to-eye look at that "now extinct" KGB security. They said that the KGB no longer existed. (If you believe that, I have some wetlands in Louisiana, I would love to sell to you.)

Upon arriving at the airport in Moscow, I experienced what it was like to be an American. As all the Americans checked in, I noticed the way they scrutinized us. The authorities wanted to know what we were doing in their country. We told them we had flown in to work on a Pizza Hut commercial with Mr. Gorbachev.

There were different reactions to that statement. Some were excited and liked Mr. Gorbachev, while others blamed him for all the changes in Russia.

Exiting the airport, we were taken to one of the most excellent hotels I have ever stayed in. It was across the bridge from Red Square. I don't remember the hotel's name, but I do remember its abundant nature and decor. This hotel catered to the world's most prosperous. I think I had the cheapest room at $600 a night. (The prices then)

One night, while in my room across the bridge from Lenin's tomb in Red Square, my television blared in the background. (Yes, they had cable TV in their rooms in Moscow then.)

The weirdest thing happened. I was watching a BBC report. Ironically, on the tube was some old footage of Nikita Khrushchev banging his shoe on a podium and screaming. Then, the news cut away to an old newsreel of the Russian army marching in front of several tanks through Red Square. I immediately looked out my window to see an empty Red Square.

It all seemed so surreal. It felt like I had entered a "Twilight Zone" episode.

The following day, we got up early and started filming our commercial. I noticed on this job that no matter where you go in today's world, motion picture grips will act like grips. The only difference between the grips and the electricians from other countries and the United States is their movie tools available for filming. It appeared to me that they have the exact same sense of humor. All my guys had great attitudes. I was lucky enough to capture a photo opportunity with Mr. Gorbachev on the Pizza Hut set.

When the commercial was over, I gave one of my grips my 9.6-volt battery-operated Makita screw gun. You would've thought I'd given this gentleman a bar of gold. I gave it as a gesture of friendship. The man's mouth literally dropped open. I don't know if he thought of Americans as capitalist pigs like we were told in the old days, much like I was told that all of them were communists in my youth. But at that very moment, we were just good friends!

Take a Powder

This is practical joking at its best. Over the years, I've become quite a practical joker, but this was one of the best ones for me.

I was sent on location to film a commercial near the Bonneville Salt Flats in Utah. It was a scorching day. When we were not filming the commercial, the client and agency reps would jump back into their rental cars and start their engines to run the air conditioners. On the first day, two people from the advertising agency said they had been warned about me and my partner in crime, José. They were told to be on the watch for practical jokes from us.

José and I acted so sweet that butter would not have melted in our mouths. After a long day of filming, everybody said good evening. They were so happy about how the commercial was filmed today that they would see us back at the hotel. José and I first jumped into our rental car and drove just out of range.

We watched the two clients from the agency get into their vehicle. When they turned over the key to start the engine, a plume of white smoke filled the entire cab. Unbeknownst to them, I had filled each of their air conditioner vents full of baby powder, ensuring no powder spilled out onto the floorboards. Then, I set the blower fan to high on the dashboard. The blower kicked in as soon as they started the car and released the key. The baby powder smoke completely engulfed the occupants. The sweet, soft smell of success!

Got the Buzz

Over the years, while working as a motion picture film technician (i.e., grip), I have had many experiences meeting various celebrities. I have a huge respect for actors and actresses, presidents, dignitaries, and now the second man to have set foot on the moon.

Not only did I film a commercial in Moscow's Red Square with Mikhail Gorbachev, but I also filmed a commercial with Clayton Moore (aka the "Lone Ranger"), my childhood idol. It was a magical dream come true. I felt like I was seven again—to stand next to him!

With my love of all thing's aviation, I dreamed of becoming a licensed aircraft mechanic after seeing Russia's Sputnik spy ship in the western sky. Now, top that with meeting a true American icon. A man with two others who had the daring to basically ride a ride, much like a Roman candle strapped to their backs. Sure, it was calculated. So were the shuttles. Meeting a genuine "Made in America" hero was an honor.

I had the honor and privilege of shaking this gentleman's hand. It was retired Colonel Edwin "Buzz" Aldrin. As I write this, I reflect on how lucky I am to be doing this job. It is a physical job, to say the least, and mentally strenuous at times, but it is an honorable, hardworking person's job.

As I've said, I'm not overly educated, but I'm no dummy either. (Some say I have street smarts.) My best two traits, as I see them, are perseverance and determination.

Esquadrão da Morte!

I did a job in an unnamed country many years ago. The local crew brought in a young man from college studying film at the university. I liked the kid. So, I showed him around the set and let him work with me for a few days. The day before we left the country, I got his father's invitation to come to his massive office to thank me for taking care of his son while on the film crew. You see, his father's company oversaw the security of our Director and Cameraman safety, who were not from this country.

When I met the gentleman, he was so pleased and kind to me for taking care of his son that he gave me his private business card and the epaulet's insignia pin off his jacket and handed it to me. Speaking through a translator and broken English, he told me, if you need anything, you have my phone number on that card. Just give me a call. Anything! Only on the flight home did I find out that this gentleman was allegedly in charge of the Esquadrão da Morte! This is true, No Hollywood B.S. (Sometimes, it's nice to be a DBL kind of guy!) (DBL – Dumb, but lucky)

How to Get in This Business!

Apply at any grip or electrical equipment rental house if one is close enough.

Be a jack of all trades if you want to survive.

Be a self-starter.

Be kind.

Be respectful to everyone!

Be passionate.

Be hard-working.

Be proactive.

Tell people you're looking for future work.

Be willing to work a few jobs for nothing until you acquire skills.

Check for filming notice at the local or state film office.

Check in with the local union hall or business agent.

Check with the permit office.

Check Craigslist.

Do an internship.

Don't be annoying.

Get a Film Degree.

Get on set as an extra or stand-in.

Have a card ready. Print the name and phone number on both sides. Why both sides? I have seen many a person uses the back of another's business card to write their info on it… to acquire future work for themselves. Print on both sides of your card because they will not write on it and will give it away in a pinch for scrap paper.

On non-union, wear different hats in different short films.

If you see film trucks in your area, try to get your resume to them.

If you want to direct, you need to make your own films.

In the beginning, try different things first and see where you land.

It doesn't magically happen on a timetable.

Join an extras agency and get the feel of a working set.

Keep a good attitude and make friends.

Be of good character and integrity.

Keep a list of everyone you meet.

Collect and give contact info.

Keep being humble.

Learn as much as you can.

Ensure people see you on set often, being busy.

Make yourself indispensable.

Never give up… never surrender. (Sounds like something from a movie I saw)

Never say no to work.

One camera person… several grips, and many electricians. Now, do the math and place your bet on yourself.

Pick a craft.

Read and watch the behind-the-scenes shorts.

Buy the grip book, the electrical book, and the camera handbook.

Save every call sheet.

Never say that you're interested in doing multiple crafts… can be a red flag. (Why would I spend time training you?)

Show up and observe.

Sign up as a permit worker.

Start as background or a production assistant.

Start your own production company.

Take the time to learn about the department that most interests you & build the skills that suit that department.

Talk to every department you're interested in.

Who You Know. Try to know everyone.

Undersell, over-deliver.

Understand that this work isn't for everyone.

These are just a few of the ways I seen or heard of. Remember, they won't answer the door if you don't knock!

Finally, Do Not sell your soul to the Devil. (But blackmail does works, I have been told! Naw... just kidding... no, really!)

Jobs People Had Before Film!

Over the years, I have asked many crewmembers what they did before they got into the movie-making business.

Bouncer.

Cabinet maker.

College teacher.

Commercial artist.

Computer school.

Contractor.

Cook.

Custodian.

Dancer.

Dishwasher

Disneyland worker.

Federal corrections officer.

Infantry soldier.

Magician.

Mailman.

Martial artist.

Microbiologist.

Moccasin maker.

Muralist.

Railroad brakeman.

Restaurant manager.

Rodeo clown – now directing- I kid you not!

Rubber factory worker.

School.

Sheep herder.

Shoeshines.

Student.

Teacher.

Trawler deckhand.

Union steward.

Who Does What on A Film Crew?

Advertising Agent - Sell words to people to try and convince them.

Art Dept - Make new things, look old.

Camera Operator - Films people.

Construction: Builds structures that are torn down and thrown in the rubbish.

Director – Tell people what to do.

Dolly Grip: Pushes around a four-hundred-pound dolly while people ride on it.

Executive Producer - Hire people they don't really know.

Grips: Scatter equipment, load the truck, go home.

PA – Hear voices in their heads.

Producer - turns money into movies.

Scenic Artist - Make unrecognizable forms with various coats of paint on them.

Screenwriter - Sometimes lies to people on paper for effect.

Set Dresser - Makes movie sets pretty.

Sound Mixer - Listen to people who say things.

Wardrobe - Make people wear someone else's clothes.

Wrap Gifts

At the end of most movies (and some TV shows), there has been a long-standing tradition of throwing the cast and crew a wrap party. At these celebrations, the production will often hand out "Wrap Gifts." Some are great gifts, some… not so much. (But hey, everything is so costly, including the expenditure of the shindig.) Production has paid the entire cast and crew for several weeks or months. So, I appreciate that they have done this traditional, ongoing, nice gesture. Of course, there may always be some crew folks who will complain about how cheap production is.

If these folks are so unhappy, my thought is: simply don't show up then. Why make themselves so miserable? To them, I merely say that "Old" Hollywood maxim, "Oh Well!"

Here are some of the gifts I have personally received or have heard from other members that they have received.

$1000.00 gift card from the lead actor.

A leather aviator jacket.

A long cruise.

A personal message was handwritten by a big-time director.

Air pods.

An Autographed script.

Australian oilskin outback coat.

Beach cruisers with the show's name on it.

Bose noise-cancelling headphones.

Car detailing gift certificates.

Carhartt jacket. (me)

Custom Pendleton blanket.

Customized Monopoly game.

Diamond earrings.

Director/Actor Autographed Slate.

Electric scooter from Curb Your Enthusiasm. (me)

Embroidered Native American blanket.

Engraved knife. (me)

Fleece-lined, hooded Carhartt jacket.

Fold up bike.

Heated vest.

High-end blue tooth battery speakers.

Bonus check. (me)

iPad.

Jacket/shirts with the show's name on it.

Leather-bound autographed script.

Money. (me) (Of course I reported it and paid taxes)

Neos overshoes. (me)

Nespresso machine.

Noise-canceling headphones.

North Face jacket.

iPad with the shows name on it.

Pocketknife.

Rolex Watch.

Several extra days of pay.

Sterling silver from Tiffany.

Three days' pay, plus hotel & per diem in Hawaii. (me)

Trip to Hawaii. (me)

Vespa.

Dog Jaw

Years ago, I was doing a lot of commercials as a dolly grip. For some reason, I ran into the same actor on three different jobs in a row. During a break, we spoke and got to know each other a bit. I felt comfortable enough to tell him one of my world-famous bad jokes. Dog jaw!

It starts out with me rubbing my jawbone at the Mandeville hinge point. The actor looked at me and asked what the problem was? I told him I had been in the service during the Vietnam War era and may have picked up Dog Jaw in the jungles. Dog jaw was his reply. I rubbed a little more and said, Yeah, sometimes it just hurts like hell.

As I rubbed my jaw for the final time, I invited the actor to feel the big knot built up over the years on my jaw's hinge point. As he reached in tentatively with his index finger, I whipped my head to the side and snapped my teeth at his pointer finger, all the while loudly screaming, **Wolf!**

He immediately retracted his hand and started to laugh, realizing he had been had. So, we had to go back to work after lunch. I was positioned on the dolly, ready to make my camera move, and he was on his start mark, prepared to do his action. As he looked at me and I at him, we both busted out in uncontrollable laughter. We laughed so hard and for so long that I was asked to leave the working set. It literally took me about 10 minutes to get over my laughing jag. The actor as well, I am told. Almost got fired for that one, but it's still an excellent memory.

Reasons for Delay of Filming

A home invasion occurred two homes away from the location.

A local angry Karen.

Background fired shots on set.

Bank robbery next to location.

Bomb-sniffing dogs.

Challenger disaster.

Crop duster one farm over.

Dumping piss on crew members.

Exploding cars.

Gang drive-by shoot-out.

Gunfire.

Gunshots at the crew.

Helicopter crash on set.

The horse in the movie had an erection.

Hundreds of rats.

Junkies are throwing used needles at the crew.

North Hollywood shootout - all on live television.

Northridge earthquake.

Piss bags are thrown at the crew.

Plane crash.

Rodney King decision day.

Several sharks showed up.

Someone dropped a frozen chicken from about 10 stories up.

Someone set off various car alarms while we were rolling.

Someone sliced the tires on the generator.

Someone threw batteries from the top of an apartment building at the crew.

Someone threw hard-boiled eggs at the crew.

Sprinklers flooded all the books at a downtown library location.

Three inmates went missing during filming.

Places That I Have Been Able to Visit Because I Became a Motion Picture Film Technician, I.E., Grip (This isn't brag, this will be you someday!)

I was hired to go to Oslo, Norway, and stay for a week of work. I drove through the snowcapped mountainous regions along the inlets. I looked at a smooth glass lake that gently reflected its surroundings on this beautiful country's crisp, cold morning. I traveled to Paris on my way home from Russia. I traveled to Argentina and Brazil to do an American Airlines commercial. I stood at the foot of the Christ the Redeemer, the Art Deco statue of Jesus Christ in Rio de Janeiro, Brazil. I just stared at Jesus with his arms wide above the lovely cityscape. I went to the Falkland Islands and did a commercial.

A few others and I literally carried a former Sports Illustrated cover model from a sandy beach in Bermuda to a bobbing boat so that her body makeup would not get wet.

I was in Gainesville, Florida, where I filmed a nearby alligator ranch containing over 275 alligators. While filming there one day, the Director and the camera assistant ran for their lives when a one-eyed alligator swam ashore and gave chase. We literally had to jump the wire fence. My legs look like a speeding centipede in a cartoon. I traveled so fast that I may have regained a few years back in time travel.

I was sent to the island of Hilo, Hawaii, and immediately got aboard a local scuba diving boat early the next day. We went underwater scouting. The funny thing is, we were doing a Chevy commercial… only on dryland. Just the perks…

I went to Mexico City to do a Nike commercial and challenged the Olympic runner, Carl Lewis, to a 100-yard dash. He gave me a 50-yard Head start... on a 100-yard dash. Easy-Peezy. (I should have put some money on that race.) He honestly beat me by 30 yards at the hundred-yard mark.

It looked like one of those slow-motion commercials, except Jabba the Hutt (me) was running against the Road Runner. I believed I was standing still when he "zoomed" past me. No kidding! It was the most surreal thing I had ever seen.

I say all this not to say, "Oh, look at me, or look at what I have done, or look at where I've been." Still, I said it to tell you, these are the on goings of a person who had no other chance in hell to do any of this form of travel emanating from how I sprang. You can and will be here if you want it bad enough.

Like the Marines, the Hollywood industry gave me another whole new life. If you get a chance, do not squander it. I have seen a few blow-ups their own chances with a slip of the tongue or a stupid wrong gesture! (Oh well!) I filmed in over half a dozen, maybe a dozen, different states, meeting the residents. 99.9% of them were terrific folks.

OMG, it sounds like I am bragging, but I am not. I am the biggest DBL guy or anybody else who knows me.

What Is A DBL Guy, You Ask? Dumb, But Lucky.

Because of the money I could now make as a film technician/i.e., Grip. I was allowed to take my wife and children to different countries and states and see how the rest of the world lived. The education for my children was ever mind-expanding. They did not believe that certain folks had lived in the most remote places and virtually had no means of escaping that situation. They had and still have beautiful memories of their travels and a great appreciation of the lives that they were offered because of Hollywood.

Remember, as a new Grip, the green bean, the newbie, you usually carry stuff. Then you learn how to work the stuff. Then you finally become in charge of the stuff. All the time, learning to work with every other department and get along. I had made a deal with myself. Wherever I work, every three weeks, my wife and children would come to visit me on location for three days or a weeklong. Sometimes, I didn't make much money after the job was over, but I made many new memories for the entire family. I no longer have the money from those shows but have some rich memories.

Once again, it's not bragging; it's about an opportunity for you. If you really want to be in this industry, you will be in this industry. I promise you that. Use the classic statement to put your mind to it, work hard. All those things are true, but the more you learn, the more you earn.

Take it from the DBL guy who quit high school and join the Marine Corps. When they asked me what I wanted to do upon enlisting, I told them I wanted to be an aircraft mechanic. I said jet repair guy! Why? Because I couldn't spell aircraft mechanic. That's the God's honest truth!

When I got to the testing phase to see if I qualified, the Marines quickly told me I was two points dumber than a fence post and would be assigned to the firefighting aircraft team. Well, I wouldn't say I like fire. So, I would study all day, getting all my military-assigned classes, and then I would go to stupid study at night for three hours.

I learned enough in those classes to barely satisfy the minimum required knowledge to be a certified aircraft mechanic. And now, I can spell aircraft mechanic. The funny thing is, out of 187 Marines and sailors, I graduated the class. (Fear of failure does that!)

Also, just as funny, to this day, I have no command of the English language, I cannot really spell well, yet I dare to attempt to write several books. One book has been in print for over 35 years; it's now on its seventh edition, A.k.a., The Grip Book. I'm now an old geezer, and my book is still in print. (Who knew?)

So, Hollywood is open to anybody who wants to get into this industry. A lot of my stories are told, tongue-in-cheek, so to speak. A lot of them are the straightforward truth. And some might be outright Bullshit.

I may exaggerate, sometimes overinflate, but I won't ever lie to you. Please wait a minute now; I sound like one of those Press Secretaries for a politician. What was that person's name again?

Old-School Filmmaking Phases You Never Hear Anymore!

Five - Dollar Friday: Write your name on a $5 Bill, drop it in a bag, and one gets pulled. The winner takes all.

Has anyone seen the changing bag? (Use to reload film magazines on location)

Blimp the camera (Use to quiet down the camera)

Champagne roll! (Champagne was served after 100 rolls of film had been shot)

Checking the gate (Check for specks of debris in the camera)

Coke and a smoke during the private blocking (meaning soda pop… No, really… I think)

Crossing (Crossing in front of the lens) Prevents startling the D.P.

Dailies (The day before work now ready to view)

Dolly grip needs the big Ubangi (Long metal extension plate)

D.P.'s got their meters out; they must be getting close.

Dutch angel (Camera rolled to 45 degrees on its side)

Films "In the Soup" (Now exposed film is being developed)

Flag on the play (Wait until it cleared)

Flashing (Taking a photo w/ flash. (It looks like a Lamp bulb may have blew-out otherwise)

French hours - (Short shooting day- no work stop for lunch)

Could you get me a Big Eye Tener (Big Light 10K)?

Get the A/B smoke (Chemical smoke)

Get the Barney (Quiets the camera. Also called a Blimp)

Get the short whip, please (Flexible extension handle for focus puller)

Got any blow? (I don't remember)

Hair in the gate (Debris in camera)

Hollywood it! (Handhold the unit in question)

How many more short ends do we have (Pieces of short film taped together)

I need to replace a carbon rod (Old time huge lamps)

I'll fax you the call sheet (Crew directions for the day)

I've spent 40 years in this business. Twenty-five years of them waiting on sound.

Insurance Takes. (One more shot… just in case)

Let's rehearse first.

Moviola (Portable projector to watch dailies)

Need to change the Magazine out!

Per Diem Envelope (Cash)

Quad time or Double Gold pay (Long gone)

Roll out (Film used up)

Smack both sides of a magazine. (Use to quiet the film)

Sound rollout.

Taking the film to Foto-Kem. (Developing it)

This is a cost-plus job. (Long Gone)

Trimming the Arc. (Replace the Carbon rod/sticks for the ample light)

Whose pager is that going off? (Replaced by iPhone)

Odd, Yet Somehow Perfect Names Fitting Crew Members Positions.

1st AC - Buzz.
1st AC - Fuzzy.
1st AC – Sharp.
1st AD - Grace.
1st AD - Rollin.
1st AD - Usher.
2nd AC - Mark.
Accounting - Bill.
AD - Yeller.
Animal Wrangler - Kat.
Anita Stitch – Costumes - Stich.
Armor - Trigger.
Armorer - Gunn.
Art Dec - Art.
Background person - Guy.
Bird wrangler - Raven.
Boom person standing in the light - Phil.
Cam Op - O'Connor.
Camera Op - Cam.
Camera Op - Iris.
Camera Op - Preston.
Camera Op - Rod.
Carpenter - Woody.
Cast driver - Sleepy.
Cat wrangler - Claud.
Catering - Chris P.
Clearances - Clarence.
Colorist - Grey.
Construction - Hammer.
Costume Designer - Polyester.

Craft service - Stu.
Crafty - Candy.
Crafty – Soupy.
Crafty- Chip.
D.P. – Dwight.
Director – Dick.
Dolly Grip - Dana.
Dolly Grip – Track.
Editor - Post.
Electric - Bill.
Electric- Justin Powers.
EMT - Justin Case.
Female dolly grip - Dolly.
Film loader - Flash.
Fire Safety Officer - Ash.
Fire Safety Officer - Char.
Generator Op - Jenny.
Genny Operator – Max.
Greens - Wilt.
Grip - Cary.
Grip - Coleman.
Grip - Sandy.
Hair - Ruff.
Hair – Styles.
Honey-wagon driver - Brown.
HR Rep - Pete Sakes.
I.T. - Guy.
Juicer - Edison.
Key Grip - Jerry Rig.
Key grip - Kahuna.
Lamp Operator - Spark.
Layout Board – Matt.
Layout Board – Neal.
Lighting Console Programmer - Buttons.
Lighting Director - Frost.
Line Producer - Hope.
Loader - Harry Gates.
Loader - Mags.
Loader Flash.
Location Manager - Scout.

Locations Manager - Cash.
Makeup - Anny Shine.
Makeup - Flawless.
Marine Supervisor- Bob.
Marine Supervisor- Wade.
Marine Supervisor- Wade.
Medic - Fester.
Medic - Payne.
On set carpenter - Woody.
Onset greens - Lief.
Onset Set Decorator - Art.
PA - Hey.
Painter - Sherwin.
Payroll - Bill.
Producer - Moore.
Producer - Paid.
Production Accountant - Penny.
Production designer - Art.
Prop Master - Hans.
Prop Master- Kit.
Pyro guy - Flash.
Script Supervisor - Notes.
Script Supervisor - Page.
Script Supervisor - Silent.
Security - Barb Dwyer.
Set costumer - Lacy.
Sound Mixer - Mike.
Sound- Mixer - Russel.
Stand by painter - Art.
Stand in - Mark.
Stand-in - Stander.
Stills... Cammy.
Stunt person - Blaze.
Teamster - Driver.
Transportation - Map.
Transportation - Van Gogh.
Transportation – Diesel.
UPM - Dick.
UPM - Slash.
Utility - Gable.

Van driver - Crash.
Wardrobe - Taylor.
Welder - Dusty.

Strange Habits You Pick Up on Set!

Always say copy.

Being compulsively punctual.

Being early to new locations.

Drinking cold coffee. It started out hot.

Expecting all food to be free.

Feeling weird when I work an 8-hour day and think it's short.

Finishing people's sentences, said one script supervisor.

Having a comfort bag in my backpack.

Hollywood minute.

Honking before I back out.

Hungry at 6-hour intervals.

I always turn the tab on my soda can 90 degrees or tear the label halfway off a water bottle. This way, it's mine.

I eat incredibly fast.

Instinctively reach for my Leatherman pliers or hip-mounted flashlight.

Make a little folded tab at the edge of a tape roll for easy starting.

Make every step count, and always have a backup for everything.

Saying "crossing" when I cross between someone and the T.V. they're watching.

Saying "flashing" when taking a photo with a flash.

Setting two additional battery-powered alarms at night, five minutes apart.

Sleeping while driving my car home.

Standing over a trash can or at the counter to eat instead of sitting.

Still, yell points! When walking through any doorway carrying anything.

Telling people to watch their backs in public so they move out.

Yell, "Hollywood!" When something is ready to be pulled up.

Yelling 'Headache' whenever you hear something fall or drop.

Some Old Hollywood Traditions

Five -dollar Fridays - All names on $5 bills get put into a drawing bucket and the winner gets all the money!

Flannel shirt Fridays - winter months.

Hawaiian Shirt Fridays - an aloha shirt day – summer.

Pizza Wednesday.

Taco Tuesdays.

Names I Have Heard Said About Less Than Lively Crew Folks

Blister: Shows up when the work is done.

Broken arrow - (producers' kid useless and can't be fired.)

Rainbow "appears when the storm is over."

Walking Eagle is too full of shit to fly.

Pigeon: flies in, shits on everything, and then flies away.

Summer Hire: They are here but have yet to gain skills and will be gone in a few weeks.

Milo: A person who's always a mile away from the work.

Black Swan- Ungraceful - a danger to themselves or others.

What Really Pisses Off the Cast & Crew!

Actors showing up late.

Actors with HUGE EGOS.

Added scenes!

Adding work because we completed the day's assigned work.

Atmospheric smoke.

Batteries are not charged.

Being crop dusted on a small set – (Someone farted as they walked by.)

Being on their phone and not paying attention.

Crew smoking in production vehicles.

Disrespected.

Food poisoning.

Four P.M. call time on a Wednesday… on the studio lot.

Fraturdays.

Grace called daily.

Honey Wagon with tiny toilets.

Insults about the crew from the cast. (or visa-versa)

La Croix.

Lousy craft service.

Minimum turnarounds.

Nine hours of work, then a company move.

No drinking water or washroom facilities at the location.

No more toilet paper or hand soap.

No parking for the crew.

No trash bins on set.

No vegan options.

People are smoking right by the set.

Safety meeting, and nobody pays attention.

Shoot the rehearsal.

Some dummy says it's going to be an early day.

Someone from a different department doing my job.

Splinter units!

Split days.

Spray painting inside the filming stage.

Surprise night scene on the schedule.

The clock that reads A.M. at the end of the day.

The director says, would, if, or could we…

The honey wagon removal tank truck always comes to empty the honey wagon at lunch time.

Unheated changing tents in winter.

Unprepared directors.

Unprofessional people.

When production assistants do not relay that it's a cut after the scene.

When the client/agency outnumbers the crew.

When your equipment truck is parked two blocks away from the set.

Me - I plead the 5th!

The Kindest Things Seen on Movie Sets

(Look, I cannot confirm all these stories, but chances are they are most likely true, maybe embellished a bit, maybe not enough. Personally, with 40+ years in now, I'd bet closer to true. Enjoy, M.)

Five-Dollar Friday (Heart-warming)

The crew writes their name on a $5 bill, then drops it into a bucket. At wrap time, a P.A. will reach into the now-raised bucket and grab a bill. The winner takes all. The production assistant drew her own name. The entire crew booed loudly. The embarrassed P.A. explained that she had not even entered the contest. So, she pulled another bill. Her name, once again, was on the second bill. The crew's boos grew louder. Now mortified, she asked to leave. The crew responded, *after* you draw the next bill.

She slowly reached in and selected another bill. OMG, her name was on the third bill. She sank to the ground. A young crew woman raced in and informed her that all the bills had her name on them. You see, she was homeless, sleeping in her car, and still going to work on time. She sobbed like a baby as she thanked everyone while giving each a (now unlawful and forbidden) hug.

P. S. There were over three months of rent in the bucket.

No "Misery"

It has been said that a certain leading actress (KB) heard that the producers from the movie production she was on had cut the budget for the crew's wrap party. That was not going to happen on her watch. She rented an entire country club on her dime. Like this story, I heard it was a fabulous party!

Country Gold

It was discovered that a crew member had been hiding his progressing cancer while still trying to earn a living for his family. The lead actor (BRS) and the J.H. band held a benefit. All the money went to help the family.

I Wish I Could Be Trading Places With JLC.

The lead actress was about to leave a restaurant when she spotted several of her departing crew in the back having a small wrap party dinner. She dropped by the table to wish them well on their future jobs and offered up a round of drinks. The final, huge bill never arrived for the crew's dinner after she left. Just a note showed up; thank you all, J. (or so it is said) (Looking good Billy Ray)

Drew The Right Day to Come to Work

As I arrived at the stage, I noticed a brand-new Benz in the lead actor's parking spot as he drove up to park his Toyota truck. He parked behind the car, blocking it in, and then quickly walked onto the stage and yelled out. Who has the crappiest car on the crew?

When a crew member finally walked up and said he had the crappiest car, D.C. threw him the keys to his truck and said, Go Park YOUR truck in crew parking. It's blocking the new Benz that production just gave me. I'll bring your pink slip in tomorrow.

No Dead Pool of Time.

The actor RR walked off the shooting set after shooting a scene, leaving the entire cast and crew puzzled. Moments later, he returned with a busload of special needs children. All the kids were overjoyed with their visit to the set. This stopped production for over an hour. R.R. anonymously picked up all the productions and special needs children's trip costs out of his pocket.

The Humble Dane

The lead actress, HM, noticed a background actor had a hard time pretending to enjoy their prop movie meal. It was a thick, juicy steak. The problem was that the actor was a Vegan. Dane H quietly and politely asked the props to exchange the food for a vegan plate in a gentle, assertive voice. Then, the scene continued.

Taking The Law into Their Own Hands

Jury duty called on a working crew member, as it does to many. The worker badly needs her paycheck to pay rent but fulfills her civic duty. When the crewperson returned five days later and received her check, she had been paid her regular pay for the entire week of jury duty. There was a note with the check. We are proud of you! Signed, Production.

Small Gestures Mean a Lot

A huge actor asked the young attendant her name while at the craft service table. Every day thereafter, the actor would graze at the table and call the craft person by name.

This Pirate Had a Bead on The Kids

An actor, J.D., had his assistant carry clips of pirate braids containing shells and beads to hand out to the kids when they recognized the famous sparrow.

Summer Rose

A craft person's mother had passed three days before the end of the show. When the lead actress heard this, she brought in a beautiful white rose to express her condolences. I was told that the actress was not scheduled to work that day, but she brought in the rose on her own time!

Pizza For All

I worked as a day player on a movie called Freedom Writers. Danny DeVito was one of the producers. He bought pizzas and sodas for the entire block of people watching the movie being filmed while standing and sitting across the street on their front porches. The scene we were filming was in front of a high school. Everyone watching was quiet, like field mice, as they ate their treats. If a noise was made, it was quickly dealt with by the self-policing viewers. It was, let's say, a rougher part of Long Beach, CA. Well played, Mr. DeVito

6-Week Chevy Commercial

I had just finished a 6-week Chevy commercial. We started in California, traveled to Chicago, and finished in Hawaii. On the last day of the commercial, the UPM handed all the crew an envelope full of cash and an added three days of a fully paid hotel stay, along with per-diam for food and drink.

Give Till It Doesn't Hurt.

There are many stories about the cast and crew worldwide. I have seen someone win a huge raffle and donate the money to someone else.

Comic Relief

I worked on one of the Comic reliefs performances. After finishing his stage set, one actor began disrobing as he left the stage. When he got down to his Comic Relief t-shirt, he removed it and threw it to my son David. It was like that famous Coke-a-Cola scene with the football player Joe Green. (It was Bobcat Goldthwaite.)

There Are a Lot of Jobs You Can Easily Do After You Leave the Movie Industry.

You can become:

An Arsonist

An Assassin

Babysitter

Barista

Bomb squad worker

Bowling instructor

Bull shit artist

Cat wrangling

Court arbitrator

Crime Investigator

Daycare worker

Demo expert

Dictator

Disaster recovery specialist

Doorman

Drug dealer

Ego massage

Events management

Executioner

Fire-person - Putting out fires

Fluffer

Furniture mover

General contractor

Gigolo or Madam

Good at asking for forgiveness

Hairstyling

Hooker

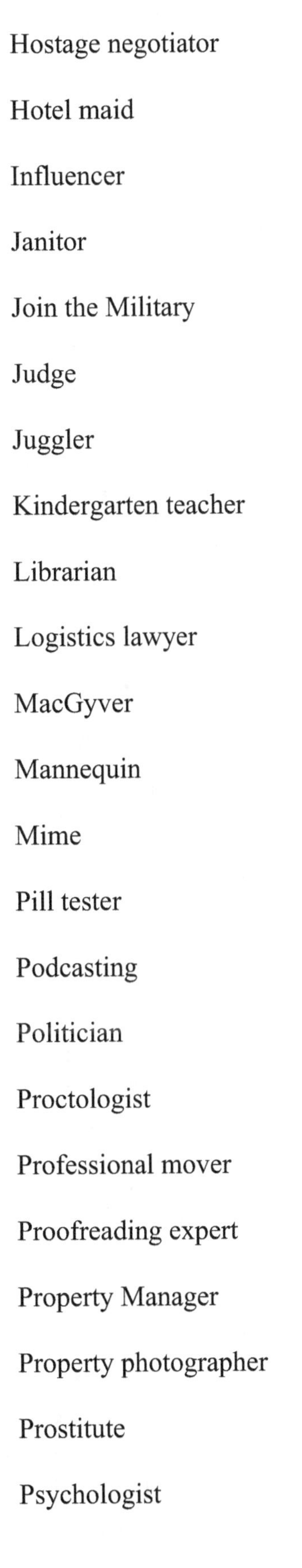

Hostage negotiator

Hotel maid

Influencer

Janitor

Join the Military

Judge

Juggler

Kindergarten teacher

Librarian

Logistics lawyer

MacGyver

Mannequin

Mime

Pill tester

Podcasting

Politician

Proctologist

Professional mover

Proofreading expert

Property Manager

Property photographer

Prostitute

Psychologist

Punching bag

Railroad yard worker

Real estate stager

Ringmaster

Ruler

Setting up an apocalypse

Sniper

Spending someone else's money

Squeeze ball tester

Stand-up comic

Start a war

Super Villain

Therapist

White collar criminal

President of the United States

A List of Old Hollywood Jokes That Are Constantly Repeated on Set

(I do not know who originally coined them, but I have heard 99% of them.)

A UPM's son walks into his office and asks his dad for $20. His dad says, what do you need $15 for? I don't have $10. Here's $5.

My shoes have more time in the honey wagon than you do on movie sets.

How many Teamsters to screw in a lightbulb? Then, you need help with that. (I LOVE the teamsters so much; I once was one.)

Once you shoot a rehearsal, it's not a rehearsal!

What two types of people do extra work? Those who don't want to work at McDonald's… and those who can't get a job there.

What's the difference between a director and a coconut? You can get a drink out of a coconut.

What's the difference between a film crew and a puppy? A puppy usually stops whining after the first couple of weeks.

What's the difference between a highlight and a flare? About $5,000 a week.

What's the difference between God and a D.P.? God doesn't think he's a D.P.!

Everyone wakes up and runs for their cars when it's a wrap.

When will you ever see a crewmember wearing a suit? When they are headed to court.

Why did the crewmember spread Cheerios in the backyard? They thought they were doughnut seeds!

Why do you not date the Script Supervisor? Because they carry a stopwatch.

Why does thunder come after lightning? Even God must wait for sound.

You are on location, not a vacation.

You're either helping me or fu*king me... but right now, you're not fu*king helping me!

Oops, "TRUE" Stories Within the Movie Industry (Who Knows for Sure)

A specific department rinsed their paint brushes in a koi pond at a private resident's home.

A crewmember, moving a vehicle, lost control and ran into a dry-docked boat on stilts. The ship rolled over, causing other boats to tumble like dominos.

A Hollywood-based crew had accidentally swamped the L.A. Central Public Library fire suppression sprinkler system. (This one is true!)

A colossal movie lamp was placed too close and aimed at a huge plate glass window. The glass popped like popcorn. (Diana's)

An adhesive used to camouflage an object in the interior of the 5th-century Basilica took the plaster off the wall while removing it. (Whoa-a, Momma-Me-a)

What happens when you drop a walkie-talkie from an 80' condor?... You are correct!

I watched horror as a C-stand fell over, hitting the Hiroshima band's most prized ancient Japanese instrument; the koto. It did leave a dent. (Saw it happen)

If you ever go to the railroad roundhouse in Sacramento, CA., do not look too closely at the pipe organs ornate wood-carved lectern that holds the sheet music. (Been there, may have done that)

My son and I were in a helicopter, extracting a techno crane from Hunt's mesa in Monument Valley, Arizona. A heavy wind gust slammed the craft. The load began to sway in an ever-enlarging circle. The pilot screamed, one more like that, and I jettisoned the load into the Grand Canyon. Twenty-five feet away from the edge of the approaching cliff, we were slammed again. The pilot guillotined the cable. It flung and fell away from the craft. We shot upwards. The Crain somehow made the lip of the bluff by four feet and fell on its side. Damage, yes, but not a loss.

So, you name it, and most likely, we broke it all by accident.

Then there is the story of a cameraperson handing off a giant Panavision camera and lens from boat to boat—it sank fast!

We were using one of the first drones to shoot a bird's eye view of a crow spotting a ridge line of a big red barn. The $70,000 Drone Helicopter unit was on its maiden flight. It looked fantastic as the unit swooped toward the ridge of the barn. The camera went faster and faster, closer and closer, finally smashing into the roof. The craft had flown just out of radio control range… oops! P.S. Whenever I watch the news and see a rocket hit a bullseye target, I have flashbacks of the crow meeting the barn. (Talk about an ECU!)

Over-The-Top Things Requested by Cast or Crew (Allegedly)

Penguins that could fly in a scene.

The actor was told to smash his face into a real glass mirror to look authentic.

An actor wanted a P.A. fired for not opening the stage door quickly enough.

Wanted the pool to be filled with Evian water.

Animal stories, anyone?

Two pythons were stored in a large cooler on set. Someone wrote and left a cardboard sign on top: Ice Cold Drinks!

A trained monkey mysteriously kept wanting to hold the script woman's hand. The trainer told her he'd only seen that once before when his wife became pregnant. On a whim, the script woman took a test that night; she had, in fact, become pregnant.

K

My former Spanish-speaking Best Boy got a big job working on a show in Mexico. They loaded a miniature mini donkey on a boat from a pier and sailed to an island without a landing. So, the local hired crew just pushed the donkey off the boat into about ten feet of water. It rolled over on its back and sank to the sand below. Once there, not moving a muscle, it slowly flipped over somehow and floated up to the surface. Once its head cleared the waterline, it swam as fast as it could to the shoreline. It disappeared into the dense jungle foliage forever.

Don't Gitty-up

Sam, the director, hopped on a picture horse for a photo op. It spooked and ran off. All the crew watched as the director's legs and arms began flailing in fear! The horse wrangler finally caught up with the horse. The director changed his clothes.

P.S. A large photo of that event is hanging on the bedroom wall in the same movie.

Notes

Did you know that a Lion can stream for over twelve feet?

In a commercial, the silver-shaded Persian, fluffy white cat was named Shit Head on the call sheet!

The best advice from the industry

Be kind and supportive.

Do the hard stuff first.

Do this one thing to succeed: don't quit.

Get caught doing at least one good thing a day!

Everything goes full circle, so watch what you say.

I only hire a crew that I want to spend time with.

If you don't know, ask!

If you don't know, say so. Then follow that with, I will find out.

If you feel on time, most likely you're late.

If you're working, don't take the phone call.

In a few years, that PA may be the executive producer.

In Hollywood, we live in a bubble. We are better paid, work with cool people, and it's a more rewarding job than most!

It's not how much you make; it's what you save. (Smart people don't eat their lunch too early!)

Keep your ego out of it.

Know the factory names of the equipment you use. There are too many what's-ya-ma-call-its and nicknames around the world.

Know when!

Learn to look at the set. See what does what, what goes where, and why? It will give you an image in your mind.

Like a quote from the book The Richest Man in Babylon, save 10% of any income.

Stay comfortable and maintain your awareness.

Never talk religion or politics… never!

Only volunteer your time for free if it will pay off.

No one wants your opinion unless they ask for it!

Photograph everything and keep a record on your phone. (I promise you, one day, it will save you.) Me, more than once!

Remember, I used to be just like you, but now I am just like me!

Show up on time. Pay attention. Keep your sense of humor.

Standing by is, in fact, work.

Stop waiting to talk.

Talk is cheap, so get it on paper.

The answer will always be no if you don't ask the questions.

There's always enough time to do it over.

There's always enough time with enough notice.

This isn't a business where we underachieve.

The louder the A.D. shouts, the slower the crew goes. (It's just physics!)

Remember, you're an hourly when someone asks for something during lunch.

When you're absolutely sure, check again.

Who do you know? No! It's, who knows you?

You better have talent if you can't screw the audience.

You can never get ready enough for the personalities you'll have to deal with in the movie-making business!

You don't pay your bills with exposure.

You never know who you will work for in the future, so be nice!

You will only be a day player for a short time if the boss respects your work ethic.

You're nothing but a sandwich if you believe you're the Hero!

Your altitude is achieved by your attitude.

Your following job interview will be decided every day before.

If you're a multi-millionaire, only tell people what you think of their work.

Hollywood Defined

Bankruptcy.

Disappointments.

Divorce.

Work injuries.

Death.

God, I love my chosen career.

Notes!

Do it right or not at all whether the job is big or small.

Camera Operators Creed: Pan, tilt, invoice!

Note: Do your job as if you're packing parachutes.

No is a complete sentence.

Parting words: Kids, stay in school, or you'll end up working long hours on a film set!

Opinions from the crews!

Beats working.

Best non-real job ever.

Hard work. Long hours. Wok weekends. Pick two.

It's an addiction!

It's like living a Chess game on a rollercoaster!

It's not for everyone.

Never piss off Transpo.

Organized chaos.

Pizza isn't an authentic second meal.

The hours are needlessly long.

The hours may be extended, but the pay is horrible!

The viewers don't give much about the crew!

There's no business-like... show business.

Think High School with too much money.

Toxic, yet I remain!

What's for chicken?

Where Narcissists flock too.

You really must want to be here.

You'll love it until you don't!

Yet, most people would secretly love to do what we do.

The Four Stages of Your Film Career.

1) Who the hell is Mike Uva?

2) We need Mike Uva.

3) We want a younger version of Mike Uva.

4) Who the hell is Mike Uva?

Myth… or not!

Catalina Islands Casino promenade was set afire by a film crew in 1985!

An old tree had been cut down because it blocked some picture frames!

In a movie about Lorena Bobbitt, someone drew little scissors on all the production signs. (The funny thing is, no one wanted to yell out, Cut!)

While the crew was on an interior on location, it was noted that some had bumped carts and lighting equipment against the walls, causing about $35,000 worth of damage to the silk wall coverings.

A fisheye lens fell from a sixty-five-foot tower. Worse, the Panavision camera was still attached.

Don't stand on a huge, expensive, boardroom wooden table with your boots on to change a light bulb!

While rigging a lamp, a crewmember smashed his head on an ornate, crystal-encrusted glass lighting fixture. When the very caring homeowner heard the noise and rushed in, he yelled, do you have any fu*king idea how expensive that lamp is?

When You Walk Off a Job! *(God's Honest Truth)*

When the cops hired to protect you are cut loose to save money.

On a six-page, non-union shoot, after 14 hours in, the crew is informed they have 4 pages left to film.

No paychecks by week three on a low-budget feature. The crew was told that the union payroll company had fouled up. So, I called the payroll office. After lunch, the Key grip was told to go back to work. His answer is just as soon as we see checks. Ten minutes later. No Checks! Then Key grip spoke again. Pack it up! Each crew member was handed the producer's personal check as we packed the gear. Key grip again, Address correctly? Producer nodded. These are the last words from the Key Grip. Better be!

Thinking it might be funny, a crewmember lit off a stick of dynamite. Good-by.

Some crewmembers left when they discovered it was an extremist political ad, not a news commercial—they had been told it was!

I work without prejudice, although there have been a few jobs I would not take. I did not agree to take them for personal reasons.

Things That Make You Feel Old on Set!

A young crewmember asked what an incandescent globe was! (An incandescent globe is an element light bulb that can no longer be sold in the USA.) (They get a past… this time.)

Ask a P A about a 1-hour photo place. (A what?)

Ask any twenty-something to name one singer in the Beatles.

The PA asked if I worked on the movie Gone with the Wind. The PA was new, so, being who I am, I answered yes. In fact, I told the P.A. that I was one of the fallen soldiers in a significant scene.

Asked: What was Buffy the Vampire Slayer about? (No, seriously)

At my age, I have been on movie sets longer than some crewmembers have been alive.

Confused look, followed by, who is MacGyver?

Easy Rider, anyone?

I called out, De Plane, De Plane. Zilch! Silence was the response. My look, really!

I have movie equipment that is older than you and is still on rent.

I was the new kid. Now I am the old guy! Who knew?

Kurt Russel, who?

Makes me feel funny when I work with a camera crew who have never worked with a film camera. (just saying)

On one show, my rain poncho was older than several crew members.

One crewmember thought that Alice Cooper was a woman.

One younger crewperson asked if they were rolling.

Prince, who's that? (So, it begins)

Some can quickly drop down and do fast push-ups. (Ain't gonna happen!)

Some crewmembers think that Here's Johnny came from the movie The Shining.

Test: Ask a P.A. what the Y2K was?

The director had to teach a teenage actress how to use an old-time dial phone.

A fax machine, what?

The other day, I explained to a younger crew member that we used to lick postage stamps. They asked which side.

Time machine stuff: What is a brute? Answer, an Arc. The second answer is an old-time, huge movie light used by motion picture studios. They were phased out for the most part upon the arrival of a lamp called an HMI!

What's a Thomas Brothers map?

When a P.A. tells you that they saw your credits on Top Gun when they were a little kid.

When a young P.A. tells you they had never heard of Mad Max.

When you meet a director, who is younger than your children.

Kind Things That Crew Do For Each Other

You can move to the head of the line because they know you are first up after lunch.

Transpo is putting fuel in your car.

Free haircuts by the hair department at lunchtime.

Helping you with their connections when you're new.

Lending you tools from their kits.

Move their gear, making some room for your stuff.

Teach you their insider tricks.

The grips will leave their ramp behind when you wrap after them.

Come to think of it, crews are good people.

Cliches And Over-Used Sayings That Are Heard in The Movie Business

Above my pay grade.

Back to one.

Bob's your uncle. (there you have it)

Brilliant!

Come, having had.

Do I really need to do that?

Film the rehearsal.

Flag on the play!

Flying in.

Going again!

I'll make it up to you on the next one.

It's an oner.

It's a simple little shot.

It's another Saturday.

It's not my first rodeo.

Living the dream.

Make it look organic.

Make it safe.

Moving on.

Next shot, night for day.

Not my job.

On my last show.

Perfect. Let's go again.

Reset and go again.

Run that up the flagpole.

Shoot the rehearsal.

That was great, let's do it again.

Five people are waiting for your spot.

This is my first barbeque.

This is where it all happens.

Waiting on a cloud.

We need to work as a team.

We'll loop it.

We're back in.

We're like family.

We'll fix it in post.

We're getting off early.

We're in.

We're not going to use it.

Cliches And Sayings That Should Be Heard More Often in The Movie Business

Boom sounds great!

The coffee truck is here.

Do you need some additional workforce?

Do you want your check upfront?

Eight and skate.

Go home and enjoy your wife and family.

Hard out by 6 pm.

House lights.

I have approved your request for a larger crew size.

It's my pleasure to have worked with you.

It's an early lunch.

May I pay you now?

Moving on.

On the Abby after lunch.

Paychecks at wrap.

Please & thank you.

Rain and thunder are expected today, so wrap it up. You're done.

Steak and Lobster again.

Sushi at Crafty.

Tacos at Crafty!

That was perfect, next scene!

That's an early wrap.

There are no notes.

This one takes us home!

Walk away wrap.

We can hit it fresh on Monday.

We will be sharing the profits.

We're on a meal penalty for the rest of the day.

We're out by noon.

Who's available for another ten weeks?

Wrap before lunch.

You available?

You're back tomorrow.

You're all getting a bonus.

You're done early. Go home.

You're hired. Start tomorrow.

Your check is here early.

POV'S
OF
CREWS

These P O V drawings is what happens when you sit on an apple box for too long and you think of all the different scenarios now you see on set. So, I had a good friend of mine draw these for me. Please don't be insulted.

the ACTOR

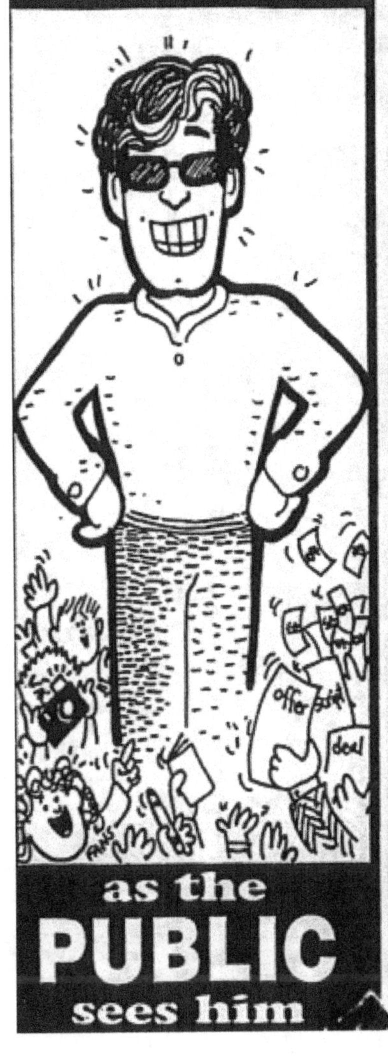

as the **PUBLIC** sees him	as he sees **HIMSELF**	as the **CREW** sees him

the ACTRESS

Hubba Hubba!
WOW!
as the
PUBLIC
sees her

STAR
A humble servant of the cinema
REVIEWS
Moving performa
Brilliant!
Variety
Heartfelt!
They love me, they really love me!
BRAVO BRAVO
CLAP CLAP
CLAP CLAP CLAP CLAP
CLAP
CFriesen
as she sees
HERSELF

get my agent on the phone
where's my ma
my motor home is too small!
I SAID SPARKLING WATER!
clear the set, I'm acting!
who lit this set, anyway?!
this dress is atrocious
How can
CREW
as the
CREW
sees her

the CAMERA MAN

as the
PUBLIC
sees him

as he sees
HIMSELF

as the
CREW
sees him

the CATERER

as the **PUBLIC** sees him

as he sees **HIMSELF**

as the **CREW** sees him

the DIRECTOR

as the PUBLIC sees him

as he sees HIMSELF

as the CREW sees him

the ELECTRICIAN

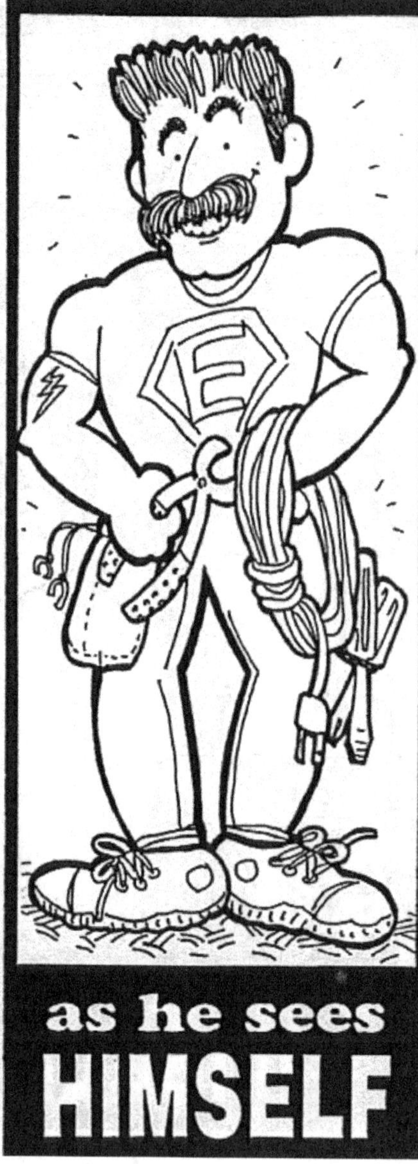

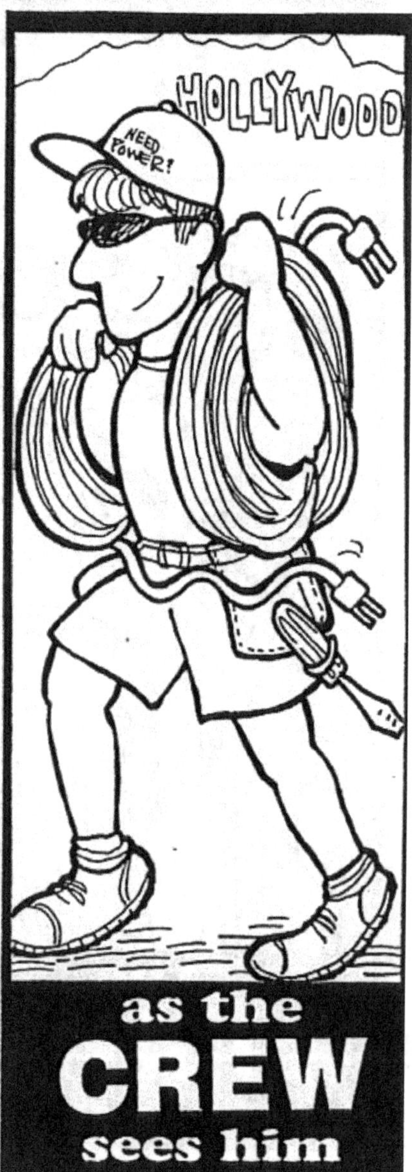

the EQUIPMENT RENTAL HOUSE

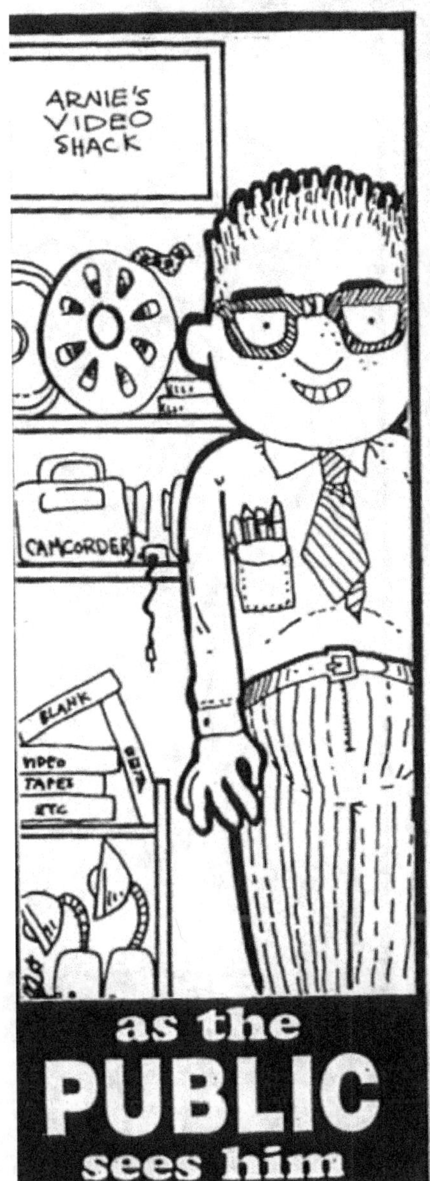

the VIDEO PLAYBACK TECH

I SURVIVED
GRIP SCHOOL
OVAVISION
THE GRADUATE
CFriesen

Future "Actress"

Future Producer

FUTURE GRIP

FUTURE STUNTMAN

TOP THAT

HOLLYWOOD Bound

FUTURE TEAMSTER
FUTURE TEAMSTER
GRIP
CAMERA
PRODUCTION
HOLLYWOOD
MINI DONUTS
HOLLYWOOD Bound

the GAFFER

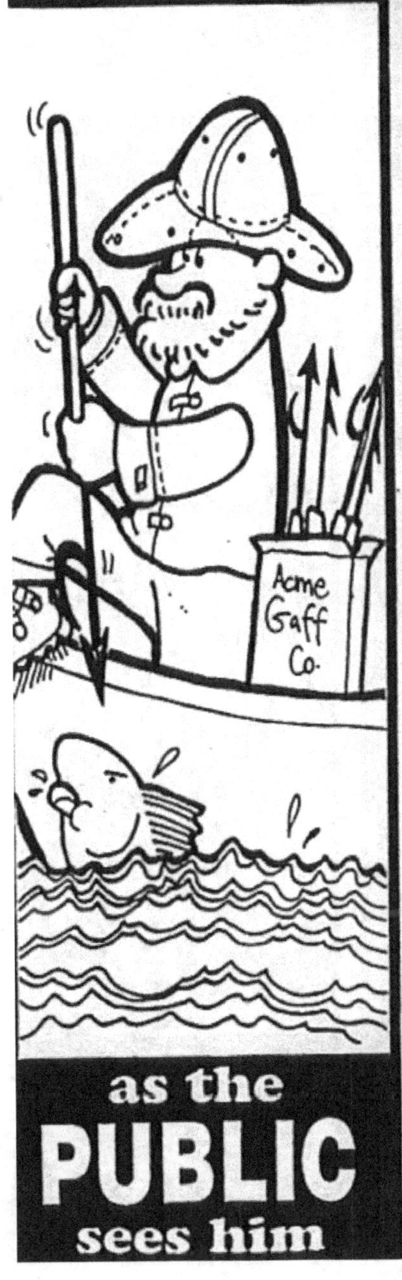

as the **PUBLIC** sees him	as he sees **HIMSELF**	as the **CREW** sees him

the GRIP

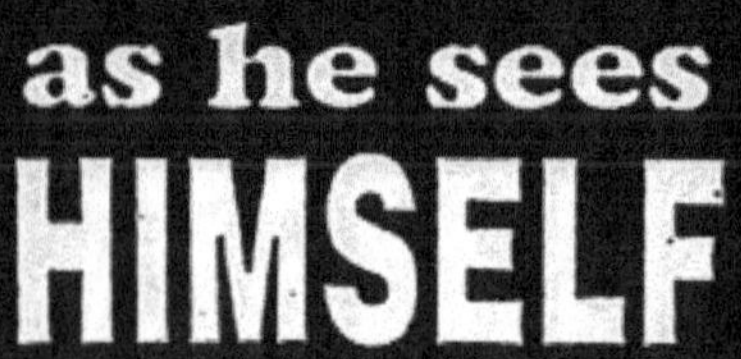

as the **PUBLIC** sees him

as he sees **HIMSELF**

as the **PRODUCER** sees him

grip

the MAKE-UP GIRL

the PRODUCER

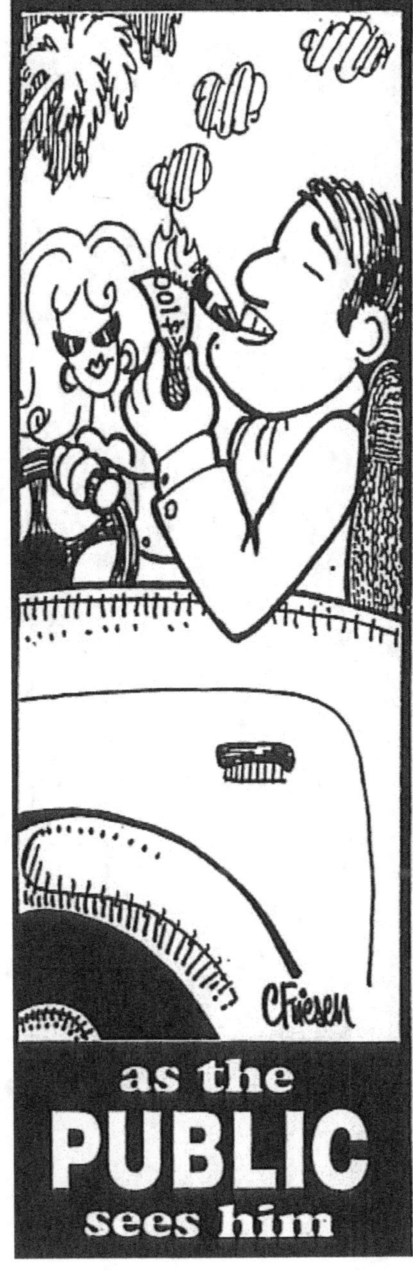

The Production Assistant

As the director sees him

As the crew sees him

As the Producer sees him

the PROP PERSON

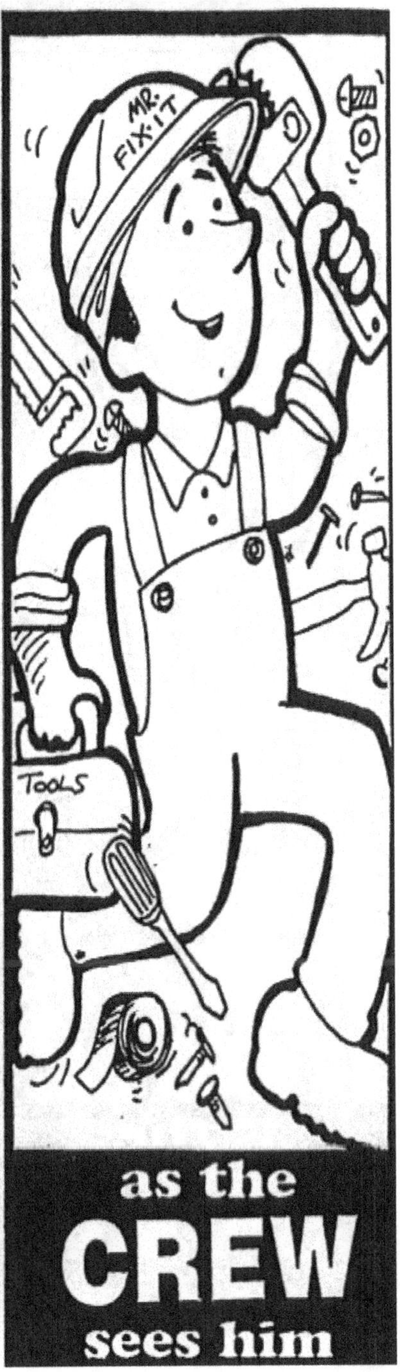

the SOUND MIXER

CIRCLE the hidden words.

```
G R I P A C P C L I E N T B I X O S E T L A O B P K Q S K L
Q V F R U E D R E T L H D C S E R J C Z W J C A T E R E R B
A A B O D A M G F S E W P P D H E F K G A M I C H Y N C M J
P R O D U C T I O N C O O R D I N A T O R M P K N G N U K L
A T B U C T R F G O T U V O G P T Y N O D R L G M R S R T X
M D U C K R O S T S R M A D H V A C T O R U W R C I R I B U
C I B T H E A E J L I D X U T Z L V Y T O K S O J P F T V G
H R D I G S F T K E C I J C N O H F W X B C P U Q R E Y H C
G E F O U S R C Q L I M P T Y A O L C M E O Z N B C D T U A
E C I N T S G O I J A K C I F B U K A N L P N D O P W X Y R
K T J M H R P M F E N S D O W Y S X M W V R H O W D Y R S P
L O M A N O L P S T U H V N Z A E B E S R O Q P G A F F E R
D R J N O I C A M E R A M A N V T C R A Y D Z A B L M K N E
O Z K A F H P N G N F I O S C E D M A K E U P N K J S I E P
O L A G E N C Y M Q V R B S D D C D A B N C H B E F O G E C
W Y L E X I S A B R I N A I F I K H S M O E G O J H U V A O
Y S C R I P T U S T B C D S R R G L S E F R T O I L N D C M
L L W X A B E V K C R A F T S E R V I C E S P M Q R D B S P
L Z S A G H A F I L M B C A O C P O S U V A M P T A M O R A
O S T U N T M A N D J M I N P T Q N T R N O U E S T A R E N
H E U B F E S X Y L O C A T I O N M A N A G E R B S N X V Y
V I D E O C T A C T I O N H K R M S N L M Q R S C R I P T B
C D I F D R E N T A L S V F H K L U T R V N K O P Q C P I D
A B O E F W R A P G W G I J P R O P P E R S O N F B Y E O O
```

CAR PREP COMPANY	GRIP	ELECTRICIAN
SOUND MAN	CLIENT	HAIR
CRAFT SERVICE	SET	PRODUCTION ASSISTANT
STUNTMAN	CATERER	DIRECTOR
LOCATION MANAGER	PRODUCTION COORDINATOR	RENTAL HOUSE
RENTALS	ACTOR	CAMERA ASSISTANT
PROP PERSON	GAFFER	WARDROBE
ART DIRECTOR	CAMERAMAN	PRODUCER
PRODUCTION MANAGER	MAKEUP	BOOM PERSON
ACTRESS	AGENCY	BACKGROUND
TEAMSTER	SCRIPT	KEY GRIP
SET COMPANY		SECURITY

This ACTOR just won an Oscar. Help him get to his acceptance speech.

Coolest Experiences!

In the island of Grenada, I did a commercial for beer company and we had the sports illustrated model who didn't want to get her body make up wet, so they asked the crew guys to carry her out to the boat and then carry her back into the island you know Sometimes you just got to take the good with the great!

Years ago, I was on a commercial and they had one of our favorite crafts ladies set up for a wonderful spread of assorted treats for the crew. This woman would always ensure that all the treats were covered from the elements sometimes she would have very fine China cut glass, filled with M & M's or pretzels or peanuts or whatever. She was so meticulous about everything. She even carried a small, cut crystal bowl for her miniature poodle. So, the grips did a drive-by of the craft service table, starting on one end and just like Locust, they traveled the length of the table, grabbing what they could, filling their pockets, filling their mouth and then racing off back to work. It was devastated in seconds. Within minutes, everything was replenished and once again, so inviting.

Funny thig was that nobody had noticed that the cut-crystal bowl full of kibbles and bits that were sitting on the ground next to the leg had somehow disappeared. Funny thing was it hadn't gone completely away. It was just relocated to sitting on top of the craft service table.

But before anybody could get to the table in time, the client and the agency the ad agency, walked up to the table, grabbed a couple of paper plates and started filling them with delights. The producer, across the set, watch in horror as the client and agency who were speaking to each other at the crafty table. She raced in charge could not stop the female client in time from reaching down, picking up a handful of kibbles and bits and popping them into her mouth.

For some reason, the producer stopped, turn towards me and gave me the side eye as she walked off in a huff. I was astounded. I was mortified! I can honestly tell you, straight to your face… I did it!

Haunted Places

Over the years you may film in a lot of strange places. I personally was making a movie called Mortuary where we had in fact filmed inside an actual Mortuary. Let me tell you, I am the biggest chicken on the planet. Yes, I did serve eight years in the marine corps and was discharged honorably as a staff Sergeant. But I still don't like spiders and snakes... Or scary places.

Listed below are ten or so places and others that I've have filmed at. There are many rumors that they may be haunted. I don't believe it. It's all just make-believe… to scare the new-bee, just like in the movies. That is of course, if you believe in those sorts of things. So, be ready if you hear that you are going to film at these locations.

Santa Fe prison.

Riverview Hospital in Coquitlam, BC.

Ambassador hotel Los Angeles.

Louisiana plantation.

Abandoned mental hospital in California.

Abandoned TN State Prison in Nashville infirmary.

Alcatraz.

Alexandria Hotel in Los Angeles.

Baltimore.

Steel works factory in Fontana.

Buffalo Central Terminal.

Camarillo Mental Hospital!

Copper Queen Hotel in Bisbee Az.

Clown Motel in Tonopah, Nevada.

Eastern State Penitentiary, Philadelphia PA.

Eloise Insane Asylum.

French Quarter, New Orleans.

Gadson Hotel, Arizona.

Greystone Mansion on Doheny Drive in Beverly Hills.

Hollywood Center.

Houska Castle, Czechia.

Https://www.courier-journal.com/.../louisvill.../9501082002/
Https://en.m.wikipedia.org/.../New_Mexico_State....
Https://en.wikipedia.org/wiki/Crownsville_Hospital_Center...
Https://en.wikipedia.org/wiki/Smallpox_Hospital
Https://valeriejardin.wordpress.com/.../a-walk-around.../
Https://www.bbc.co.uk/sounds/brand/m000psj8

Set Culture That Is Sometimes Normal… On Set

Announcing to everyone when you're going to the head.
Averting eye contact.
Being rude and or cruel in the way people speak to one another.
Calling clothes pin a C-47!
Complaining about free food.
Food waste.
Free sandwiches.
Getting a coffee truck at midnight and being excited about it.
Having 'breakfast' and saying "Good Morning" to people at 6PM just before you start your overnight shift.
Leaving your trash everywhere.
Mismatched socks.
Scarfing a meal down over a trash can.
Spit buckets.
That 10 hr. days are considered short.
The AD being nasty to background.
Throwing away wood.
Working 18hr days and somehow thinking that's normal

Cheap Wrap gifts
A T-shirt.
Dog tags engraved with the show name and date.
Patches.
Stickers!

Old School Filmmaking Phases

A cowboy shot frames the actor from the knees or mid-thigh to just over the top of the head.

Back up on the mag. - move the camera the same way that the magazine is facing.

Barney. - A cover for the camera to reduce the sound that the camera makes during filming.

Black bags. - Plastic bags at the rules of film would come in inside the steel metal cans.

Bring in a Billy Barty. - A very short stand used to hold a lamp or grip flag

Burning feet. - Means that the camera is still rolling and you're just wasting the film.

Camera carpet. - A four foot by 4-foot piece of carpet used to put the camera tripod sticks on

Cameras on a reload. - changing the mag slash adding new film

Canada - WRAP = Window Shot. WRAP = USA Martini Shot.

Changing bag. - a double walled bag that the film would be changed inside of a magazine not permitting any light inside.

Chicken in the grate. - Means to check the gate inside of the camera.

Cloth tape measure. Lawn tape measure beloved by many camera assistants.

Come having had. When you show up for work you have already had your meal.

Continuity polaroid. A snapshot of what the set look like in between takes.

Cost plus. - Whatever the actual cost of the job is plus say 35% markup will be your bill.

Counting the wedges - (having a beer)

Cut, print, wrong location. - New deal - moving to another location

Day for night. - means to shoot during the day but make it look like it was filmed at night.

Drop a lavender in it. - reduce the light intensity by 10 to 15% with this thin net.

Film cores. - This spools that hold the film.

Flashing! - when taking a continuity photo with a Polaroid.

Fly an Elvis or Liberace. - a flashy silver and gold reflective material that were like the coats that Liberace and Elvis would wear during a performance.

Foot Candles. - A measurement of light intensity

Force Call. - The crew did not get their full 10 hours off before they had to come back to work so they must be paid additional money.

Fuller's Earth. - Diatomaceous earth. That powder that you put in the old-time pool filters. We use it for blowing dust here in the film industry.

Golden Time. - your hourly pay is doubled

Groucho off that. This means to move an object or person out of the way once the camera no longer sees them so they can push in through a crowd.

Hair in the gate. - those are the little scratches that you've seen on old movies all the time. They are referred to as hair.

Hertz Meter! - A tool used for measuring electricity.

John Wayne shot - frame below the holsters up.

Last looks! - This is when the hair department and makeup department come in and puts finishing touches on the actors just before filming.

Let's have a rehearsal.

Mag jam. - the film would get jammed up inside of the magazine.

Magic Hour! - That beautiful time of day sort of a reddish sunset. We would film between 3:30 PM and 6:30 PM to have that beautiful background sky. You can also do it in the morning.

Mickey Rooney (ie a little creep). - To push the Dolly at a very slow pace.

MOS - Mit out sound.

Need a Gary Coleman. – A 20-inch C Stand.

Night premium. - Paid extra money to work nights

No hammer, no callback. - Means, show up with all your tools

Noes Lube - Assistant would rub their finger on their nose, and then lubed the camera gate.

Not my rice bowl. - means, do your own job not mine

Obie light. A small lamp attached to the top of the camera. You look like and lamps on top of news cameras.

One more for Lloyds. - Lloyds of London - means one more shot for insurance.

Pulling the movement - the mechanism that pulls the film through the camera.

Push one stop. Means to increase the exposure of the film allowing more light.

Quad Time (four times the rate)

Quick sticks.

Rain premium.

Road sodas! – Beer

Roll out. - when the camel would roll out of film doing a take.

Runner to bring the film to the lab. Get the exposed film to the laboratory to have it developed before the development company shuts down for the evening.

Rushes (dailies) after wrap?

Save tail - print till end. Print all film that has been exposed to the camera.

Set up the Moviola for dailies. a portable, yet very heavy, machine that would show what was just shot the day before.

Shake em up. - Move the shiny boards and check to see where the reflection is hitting.

Shoot the Gray scale. - Ensuring that the colors are correct when shooting black and white.

Short end. - unexposed, usable film.

Squib the actor - Explosive devices that look like bullet holes attached to the actor.

Straight in on the mag.

Striking! - turning on a light.

Stuffing the Bird. - Reloading the camera

Summon the meat puppets. - call the actors to the set to film.

Teamster wallet. - a very heavy sandbag.

The mag is dishing. Smack it. the film inside the magazine is wavering side to side.

Thomas guide. Long before GPS.

Travel time. Paid to travel.

Trimming an arc! - adding a carbon rod to an old-style movie lamp. When the two rides came together they would arc and broadcast a gigantic light.

Turn Over. - roll the camera.

Upside down slate. - slam the slate together upside down at the end of the scene in case you didn't catch it at the beginning of the scene.

 Upstage and Downstage - Upstage meaning away from camera. Downstage meaning closer to camera. This s from when stages had a rise in the back so the audience could see everything.

Warner Brothers. - a very tight shot on an actor or actress's face.

Wash your back (coming through get out of the way)

Watch your eyes" when a key light is switched on.

Weekend Premium. - paid extra money to work on weekends.

Western-reload! - like the quick draw of old days, the camera would be reloaded very fast.

What's for chicken? - the film industry seems to eat chicken 365 days a year.

Worrel head. - a device used to pan and tilt the camera.

Wrap beer. - those days are long gone.

Hollywood is stranger than fiction. (Guaranteed true!)

If I had not seen it for myself, I would not have believed it. (My Boys Town story comes to mind.) Come to think about it, I can't believe what I did see… and what I did! (All… very legal of course.) See, fresh butter will not melt in my mouth.

This book is written by an anonymous source! (I don't want to get sued!) But this source has over forty plus years on movie sets and is still going strong. But I can legally tell you, the writer is a Retired Key grip.

Note:

You can always tell a grip. Problem is, you cannot tell them very much!

BTW, "What the hell is a grip anyways?" See, you really do need to read this book.

HOLLYWOOD

THE END!

Check out *MIKE UVA's* other books on Amazon:

1) **The Grip Book: The Studio Grip's Essential Guide 7th Edition:** ISBN-13: 978-1138571396 - ISBN-10: 1138571393

2) **Uva's Guide to Cranes, Dollies, and Remote Heads** 1st Edition: ISBN-13: 978-0240804873 - ISBN-10: 0240804872

3) **Uva's Rigging Guide for Studio and Location** 1st Edition: ISBN-13: 978-0240803920 - ISBN-10: 0240803922 - FEB 18, 2018

4) **Tippy: (Tales of Flying Sergeants) Enlisted Fighter Pilots in WWII Paperback – January 5, 2015, ISBN-10: 1506015832 - ISBN-13: 978-1506015835 - Jan 5, 2015**

5) **Hell On Heels! Cover B: She's the Devils Daughter Looking to Collect!** (If you think the Devil was evil, try dealing with his progeny!) Hell On Heels! (Lilith!) Book 1 Kindle Edition – Feb 21, 2015

6) **E-Jipped!** – Mar 11, 2015

7) **Chief** – July 3, 2016

8) **Breaking Into the Movies! - From Inglewood to Hollywood!** *What Really Happens Behind the Lights and The Long Road to Get There!* July 6, 2015

9) **Spray: Girls Don't Surf!** - Feb 15, 2015

10) **Hollywood Trivia: Hollywood Trivia with Insider Jokes - Sept 8, 2014**

11) **Crew Speak – Sept. 19, 2014**

12) **Fade Out: Nothing but Smoke and Mirrors!** - April 11, 2015

13) **Nirvana: Cause and Effect**: The Exchange, Book 1 - **Jul 1, 2016**

14) **Uva's Shorts: A Selection of the Finest Stories Ever Told...or not!** July 6, 2016

15) **Film Dollies-Cranes-&-Camera Heads from Around the World by Michael G. Uva (2014-09-13)**

Once upon a time…

Once upon a time, in the glitzy world of Hollywood, where dreams are spun into silver screens, there lies a hidden reality that only those behind the cameras genuinely understand their lives a passionate filmmaker named Michael Uva. For over forty-five years, he has dedicated his life to the art of motion pictures production, not just as a grip but as a storyteller who lives and breathes every frame, he has been part of. His journey so far has been a rollercoaster of experiences, revealing the unvarnished truth of what really goes on behind the scenes. So, Mike decided to pen a tell all memoir titled; "Hollywood BS- Behind the Scenes." The book is a candid exploration of his journey, filled with anecdotes that captured both the magic and madness of filmmaking. Upon its release, Hollywood BS has resonated with industry veterans, apprentices, and the public at large sparking conversations about the realities of the film world. Mikes stories highlight the triumphs and tribulations, the laughter and tears, and the unbreakable bonds forged amidst the chaos. It has become a testament to the unsung heroes behind the scenes, celebrating their dedication and resilience. His story was not just about the industry; it was a celebration of the human spirit, creativity, and the enduring power of storytelling.

Read what's been said:

A must-read book if you want to make movies.

It's about everything you may have missed in other B.S. Books.

A humorous and tear-jerking collection of true-life experiences in Hollywood.

It contains a ton of true (and a few questionable) stories.

The nuts-and-bolts of everyday lives of the cast and crews on set.

The struggles and joys of being in a Hollywood life.

Several perspectives of the crew's life in a film career.

It shows the balance between the creative forces used daily.

As seen from the other side of the proverbial fence.

Hopefully, it will be the most entertaining book you have read in years.